D0076066

THE DRAWINGS OF LOUIS HENRY SULLIVAN

Sullivan, Louis Henry

720
Su54

❖ THE DRAWINGS OF ❖
Louis Henry Sullivan

A CATALOGUE OF THE FRANK LLOYD WRIGHT

COLLECTION AT THE AVERY ARCHITECTURAL

LIBRARY ❀ ❀ ❀ BY PAUL E. SPRAGUE ❀

WITH A FOREWORD BY ADOLF K. PLACZEK

❀ ❀ PRINCETON UNIVERSITY PRESS ❀ ❀

Copyright © 1979 by Princeton University Press
Published by Princeton University Press, Princeton, New Jersey
In the United Kingdom: Princeton University Press,
Guildford, Surrey

ALL RIGHTS RESERVED

Library of Congress Cataloging in Publication Data
will be found on the page following the Index.

This book has been composed in Linotype Times Roman

Printed in the United States of America
by Princeton University Press, Princeton, New Jersey

TO MY PARENTS,

Paul Edward Sprague
AND
Miriam Drake Sprague

99047

99047

IN ORDER TO understand the full historical and artistic importance of the drawings which
we are proudly presenting in the following pages, one would first want to go back to a
scene which—as reported by one of the two participants—occurred in a shabby hotel in
Chicago on April 14, 1924. A dying architect sat in a wheelchair in his room. Once
highly successful, he was now practically forgotten. For the last time he was visited by
one of his former draftsmen, a man who had since become a very great architect. Feeling
that he was with the only one who shared his vision, the older man turned to the younger
and gave him his beloved portfolio of sketches.

Louis Henry Sullivan (1856-1924) has taken his rightful place in history as one of
the pioneers of modern architecture, as the leading spirit of the Chicago School, as the
formulator of the principle of "form follows function," and as the "lieber-meister" of
America's most eminent architect, Frank Lloyd Wright, his visitor on that April day.
Sullivan's fame thus rests not only on his architecture—his masterly high office buildings
such as the Wainwright Building in St. Louis and the Guaranty Building in Buffalo, his
various buildings in Chicago, his highly original banks in the Middle West, his exquisite
tombs—it rests equally on his eloquent and frequently prophetic writings. One thinks of
Kindergarten Chats above all but also of his *Autobiography of an Idea* and *Democracy: A Man-Search* as well as his many essays. His fame rests also on his genius as a
master of drawing, particularly as a designer of ornament. The plates of his last work,
A System of Architectural Ornament (preserved at the Burnham Library in Chicago),
are of the highest artistic value. The same may be said of the drawings owned by the
Avery Architectural Library of Columbia University, which are now published in this
volume.

Over much of Sullivan's life and work there ruled an unlucky star. Many of his fine
buildings have been or are about to be demolished by the barbarians. The destruction
of most of his architectural sketches (reputedly by his over-tidy assistant George Elmslie)
is another, almost gratuitous piece of artistic misfortune. Sullivan himself was quite
aware of the aesthetic value of even his most casual sketches. In fact, he kept the portfolio
with him even in his grim last days, much as a poet would keep his unpublished personal
poems in his desk. Frank Lloyd Wright describes the final scene—farewell and gift of
the drawings—in moving words. According to Wright, the drawings were for Sullivan
"the dearest treasure of his heart." He wanted Wright to publish them and twenty-five
years later this is exactly what Wright did in his book *Genius and the Mobocracy*. He
published thirty-nine of them, together with an account of Sullivan as a teacher, artist,
and friend. From then on, not only the existence, but also the extraordinary quality of
these drawings was known although the majority of them remained unpublished in
Wright's possession. Throughout the years it was hoped that his legendary collection
would eventually find its way into an institution where it could be made available for
scholarship, enjoyment, and, most of all, for publication *in toto*. The Avery Architectural
Library of Columbia University, with its already rich holdings of Sullivan material

(including the manuscripts of his *Kindergarten Chats* and *Democracy: A Man-Search*, his early notebook, and seventeen architectural drawings) seemed the logical place for its ultimate repository. Wright's collection was acquired in 1965, six years after his death, from the Frank Lloyd Wright estate through the generous financial support of the Edgar Kaufmann Charitable Foundation. It was in view of Avery Library's Sullivan holdings and its position as the country's greatest architectural library that Mrs. Frank Lloyd Wright and the Wright Foundation decided to entrust the treasured collection to Columbia University—122 drawings in all, to which three were added later.

The collection ranges from the early and rather rigid pen drawings of 1873-1876 from Sullivan's days at the École des Beaux Arts in Paris to drawings in 1907 and one sketch dated 1910. The majority of the drawings, however, were executed between 1885 and 1895 when Sullivan was a partner in the flourishing firm of Adler & Sullivan (Sullivan had joined Dankmar Adler as a full partner in 1883, but the firm reached its zenith of success around 1890). This was the period of his finest buildings, the most successful and creative period of his life. The years from 1888 to 1893 were also the years when the young Wright was his draftsman and "right-hand man," truly a great time for American architecture. The drawings of these years—and the later ones after his unfortunate break with Adler in 1895—are (except for two ink sketches of 1899) all pencil drawings and all freehand. Most of them are of rare beauty. Their delicacy, precision, lightness of touch and complexity, their "rightness" are immediately apparent. Among them are a corbel for the Chicago Auditorium, plaster bands for the proscenium of the rebuilt McVicker's Theater, and an exquisite sketch on office stationery of a never-built skyscraper, the Eliel Building, which reveals in one thrilling glance what took shape in Sullivan's mind at the inception of a project. Several of the drawings are annotated by Wright, either with crop notes for his intended publication or with such historically interesting comments as "beginning of the plastic period."

Avery Library's Frank Lloyd Wright collection of Louis Henry Sullivan drawings (as it has been designated) is thus of unique value and interest on several grounds: first, for the sheer beauty of the drawings themselves; second, for their insight into Sullivan's genius and its development; and third, as a document of a friendship between two great men who together fashioned America's breakthrough to architectural leadership. It is an exciting moment indeed to see these drawings at last published in their entirety.

Adolf K. Placzek
AVERY LIBRARIAN

April 1977

ACKNOWLEDGMENTS

Without the unfaltering encouragement and generous assistance of Adolf Placzek, this book would never have appeared. It was through his efforts that the Wright collection of Sullivan drawings went to the Avery Architectural Library of Columbia University. He was the person who conceived the idea of publishing these drawings and it was he who asked me to provide for them the introductory essay and catalogue that follow. To his untiring enthusiasm for the project during the years from inception to completion must be attributed its ultimate success. During those years he shepherded the project through the labyrinthine channels of the publication process, while also acting as editorial adviser whenever needed. For all of this, and for his patience, kindness, and generosity on innumerable occasions, I owe Adolf Placzek my deepest and most sincere thanks.

I want also to pay special tribute to three scholars whose kind assistance and inspiration during my work on this book is gratefully acknowledged: Donald Egbert, Hugh Morrison, and Henry-Russell Hitchcock.

To William Alex, whose guidance during the early years of writing was especially helpful, I am particularly indebted. Special thanks also go to my former student, Jack Reed, who assisted in recording the drawings, and to Thomas Yanul, who made photographic enlargements of many of the comparative illustrations.

Grateful acknowledgment is made to the following for permission to publish certain items among the comparative illustrations and for supplying the photographs:

The Art Institute of Chicago, Figs. 1, 14-15, 63
The Avery Architectural Library of Columbia University, Figs. 2, 12, 41-42, 57-58, 61
The Chicago School of Architecture Foundation, Fig. 62
George W. Furness, Fig. 7
Wilbert Hasbrouck, FAIA, Figs. 59-60
The Michigan Historical Collections, Bentley Historical Library of the University of Michigan, Figs. 3, 8-11, 13, 54, 56
The University of Michigan Museum of Art, Fig. 36
The Museum of Modern Art, Figs. 33-34
Tim Samuelson, Fig. 48
Southern Illinois University at Edwardsville, Fig. 40 (photo: John Celuch)
John Vinci, of the Richard Nickel Committee, Fig. 30 (photo: Richard Nickel)

Paul E. Sprague

CONTENTS

LIST OF CATALOGUE DRAWINGS

Sixteen drawings in the Catalogue are not by Sullivan. They are 31, 36, 39, 43, 47-50, 54, 56, 116-121. Of these the last six were drawn by George Elmslie.

No. 1. Study of a Flame. Pencil. c. 1872.

No. 2. Fresco Design [?]. Purple ink. 1873.

No. 3. Fresco Design [?]. Purple ink. 1873.

No. 4. Fresco Design. Purple ink. November 29, 1874.

No. 5. Fresco Design. Ink. April 1, 1875.

No. 6. Fresco Design. Ink. April 1, 1875.

No. 7. Fresco Design. Ink. July 11, 1875.

No. 8. Fresco Design. Ink. July 11, 1875.

No. 9. A Nude Figure. Pencil. April 1, 1880.

No. 10. A Nude Figure. Pencil. May 30, 1880.

No. 11. A Nude Figure. Pencil. November 17, 1880.

No. 12. Column Capital, Wineman House, Chicago, Ill. Pencil. c. July, 1882.

No. 13. Interior Wall with Boxes, McVicker's Theater Remodeling, Chicago, Ill. Pencil. January 9, 1883.

No. 14. Ornamental Design. McVicker's Theater Remodeling, Chicago, Ill. Pencil. May 6, 1884.

No. 15. Ornamental Study. Pencil. April 13, 1885.

No. 16. Ornamental Study. Pencil. April 18, 1885.

No. 17A. Ornamental Study. Pencil. April 18, 1885.

No. 17B. Ornamental Study. Pencil. April 18, 1885.

No. 18. Ornamental Study. Pencil. April 18, 1885.

No. 19. Ornamental Study. Pencil. May 17, 1885.

No. 20. Ornamental Study. Pencil. August 23, 1885.

No. 21. Ornamental Study. Pencil. August 23, 1885.

No. 22. Ornamental Study. Pencil. August 28, 1885.

No. 23. Ornamental Study. Pencil. December 18, 1885.

No. 24. Ornamental Design. Pencil. September 30, 1885.

No. 25A. Cover Design, Wholesale Druggists' Catalogue. Pencil. c. 1887.

No. 25B. Cover Design, Wholesale Druggists' Catalogue. Pencil. January 25, 1887.

No. 26. Ornamental Corbel, Auditorium Building, Chicago, Ill. Pencil. July 23, 1888.

No. 27. Ornamental Corbel, Auditorium Building, Chicago, Ill. Pencil. 1888-1889.

No. 28. Mosaic Stair Landing, Auditorium Building, Chicago, Ill. Pencil. 1888-1889.

No. 29. Mosaic Stair Landing, Auditorium Building, Chicago, Ill. Pencil. 1888-1889.

No. 30A. Mosaic Wall Decoration, Auditorium Building, Chicago, Ill. Pencil. 1888-1889.

No. 30B. Mosaic Decoration [?], Auditorium Building, Chicago, Ill. Pencil. 1888-1889.

No. 31. Newel Post, Auditorium Building, Chicago, Ill. Pencil. Not drawn by Sullivan. 1888-1889.

No. 32. Ornamental Capital, Auditorium Banquet Hall, Chicago, Ill. Pencil. April 15, 1890.

No. 33. Ornamental Capital, Auditorium Banquet Hall, Chicago, Ill. Pencil. July 10, 1890.

No. 34. Ornamental Capital, Auditorium Banquet Hall, Chicago, Ill. Pencil. July 17, 1890.

No. 35. Ornamental Panel. K.A.M. Synagogue, Chicago, Ill. Pencil. June 19, 1890.

No. 36. Ornamental Design. Pencil. Not drawn by Sullivan. c. 1890.

LIST OF CATALOGUE DRAWINGS

LIST OF COMPARATIVE ILLUSTRATIONS

INTRODUCTION

INTRODUCTION

THE EXQUISITE drawings of architect Louis Henry Sullivan, bequeathed at his death to his friend and former draftsman, Frank Lloyd Wright, and now preserved in the Avery Library of Columbia University, possess a value and appeal far beyond their obvious significance as documents of Sullivan's life and work.[1] As personal artistic expressions of a creative genius, they are worthy of our attention for their aesthetic qualities alone. In many of them we have the artist's original inspiration in a pure state, unaffected by the vagaries of re-drawing or, when executed, of modeling, casting, or carving, or of weathering. Studying them, we can follow the conception of each idea as it arose in Sullivan's mind and was translated into visible form by his quick and skillful manipulation of the pencil. These graphic essays form the perfect introduction to Sullivan's larger world of architectural design.

Except for a few miscellaneous drawings, Sullivan worked almost exclusively in pencil.[2] His affection for the medium can be traced to the example of his parents, from whom he received his earliest instruction in graphic expression. Their numerous pencil sketches are preserved in several collections.[3] Those by his father are nearly all outdoor scenes (Fig. 2), while the ones by his mother include, besides landscapes (Fig. 1), drawings of flowers and groups of people (Fig. 1).

No doubt Sullivan continued to work primarily in pencil because he found it the most congenial medium for recording his architectural and ornamental visions. Sullivan's temperament and the nature of his inspiration demanded a convenient medium of expression, so that the moment an idea came to him he could set to work putting it down. It was surely for the same reason that Sullivan discriminated very little in selecting paper and appears to have been content with whatever paper was within easy reach. Many drawings, such as his elegant sketch of 1894 for a tall building (No. 79), were made on office stationery. For others, Sullivan used any scrap of paper at hand. His impressionistic design for the cover of a Chicago musical magazine (No. 105) was drawn on the back

[1] Louis Sullivan was born in Boston, September 3, 1856, and died in Chicago, April 14, 1924. He was educated at the Boston English High School graduating in 1872. In 1872-1873 he studied architecture at the Massachusetts Institute of Technology and in 1874-1875 at the École des Beaux-Arts in Paris. During the summer of 1873 he worked in the Philadelphia office of architect Frank Furness and in 1873-1874 he was employed by Chicago architect William Le B. Jenney. From 1875 until 1882, when he entered a partnership with Dankmar Adler, he worked for various architects in Chicago. The famous firm of Adler & Sullivan was founded in May 1883 and dissolved in July 1895. After that Sullivan practiced alone until his death. The standard work dealing with Sullivan's architecture is Hugh Morrison, *Louis Sullivan*. For Sullivan's life see Willard Connely, *Louis Sullivan as He Lived*, and Louis

Sullivan, *The Autobiography of an Idea*. (See the Bibliography for facts of publication.)

[2] The only post-1876 drawings by Sullivan not in pencil are two pen-and-ink studies made in January 1899 for an ornamental cast-iron fence (Nos. 109 and 110). A number of pen-and-ink drawings survive from the years 1874-1876. Some are caricatures; the others, all in the Avery collection, are compositional tracings in pen-and-ink taken from pencil originals (Nos. 4-8). The only early pen-and-ink drawing not on tracing paper is in the Sullivan collection of the Burnham Library at The Art Institute of Chicago. That drawing, dated May 1876, appears to be the design for a ceiling fresco.

[3] The largest number of drawings by Sullivan's parents are in the Burnham Library of The Art Institute of Chicago. The rest are in the Avery Library at Columbia University.

of a restaurant check. A hastily improvised study for a country club, complete with plan (No. 106), was jotted down one day in 1898 on the back of Sullivan's two-by-three inch business card.

It was obviously only with the pencil that Sullivan could so easily produce the modulations of line and tone which his graphic aesthetic demanded. The delicate rhythms of fine line, darker hatchings, rollings, and scribblings, and still darker heavily-pressured points of graphite yielded a gossamer effect that was intimate and personal. Sullivan's earliest somewhat heavy-handed angular pen-and-ink drawings made in 1875 (Figs. 4-8) while a student in Paris suggest how unsuited that medium was to his temperament.[4]

The care which Sullivan took to provide each of his drawings with an exact date was also inspired by his parents, who almost always dated their own work. That the concern of all three for chronology was not merely egotism is demonstrated by the many times they thought to append the date while neglecting to sign the drawing. Had Sullivan dated his drawings out of conviction that they would some day be collected as works of art or as documents of the work of a world-famous architect, he would surely have signed them all.

ORNAMENTAL DRAWINGS

THE SOURCES. Sullivan's early ornamental designs derive from an innovative phase of the Gothic Revival that began about 1860 according to Charles Eastlake in his history of that movement.[5] This new phase, which paralleled but did not replace the historically correct kind of Gothic prevalent in the 1840's and 1850's, introduced a more original quality into the Revival. It was first seen in the stylized yet still naturalistic details of such buildings as George Edmund Street's St. James the Less at London, 1860-1861 (Fig. 5) and William Slater's Digby Mortuary Chapel at Sherborne, Dorset, 1860 (Fig. 4). In the decorative details of both buildings there are numerous designs that forecast the stylized botanical compositions of Sullivan's drawings of 1873-1876 (Nos. 2-8), for fresco-secco decorations in Chicago buildings.

Although Sullivan's conventionalized floral designs may thus be traced to the decorative work of English architects of the 1860's, his immediate sources were closer to home. The schematized botanical ornaments that decorated the buildings of the Philadelphia architect Frank Furness (Fig. 6), for whom Sullivan worked in 1873,[6] are very similar in many of their compositional patterns and specific details to Sullivan's fresco-secco drawings of the mid 1870's. The numerous parallels between Sullivan's ornament and the

[4] Although these appear at first to be tracings of caricatures in *Le Journal Amusant* the sizes of these drawings do not correspond exactly to the originals and thus were evidently drawn freehand. Six drawings of this kind are in the Burnham Library at The Art Institute of Chicago; another is in the Emil Lorch Papers in the Michigan Historical Collections at the Bentley Historical Library of the University of Michigan, Ann Arbor, Michigan.

[5] Charles L. Eastlake, *A History of the Gothic Revival* (London, 1872), Chapter XVIII, especially pp. 319-21.

[6] Frank Furness (1839-1912) received his architectural training in the office of Philadelphia architect John Fraser and in the New York atelier of Richard Morris Hunt. In 1867 he associated himself with John Fraser and George Hewitt in the architectural firm of Fraser, Furness and Hewitt. When Louis Sullivan worked for Furness during the summer and fall of 1873, the partnership had become Furness & Hewitt. For Furness see James F. O'Gorman, *The Architecture of Frank Furness* (Philadelphia, 1973).

architectural decoration of Furness make it clear that Sullivan's ornament came directly from Furness and, through him, from earlier ornament by English architects.

Intellectually, Sullivan's ornament is founded on the writings of such mid-century architectural and ornamental reformers as A.W.N. Pugin and Owen Jones.[7] These writers argued for an ornament of conventionalized motifs based on the aesthetic principles embodied in botanical form. As a source of such principles of design, Sullivan himself would recommend the study of Asa Gray's *School and Field Book of Botany*.[8] That Sullivan did not recommend the book as a source of ornamental motifs is clear from his own method of constructing ornamental compositions as it is revealed in a drawing of 1876 now in the Michigan Historical Collections (Fig. 11). The drawing seems to show an ornamental design in the process of being born from conventionalized botanical types since the labels accompanying it—"monadelphous stamen & pistels" [stamens and pistels united into one set by their filaments], "monopetalous 6 cleft corolla" [a flower composed of a single petal with six subdivisions in it], and "Navillus" [shaped like a boat]—refer to botanical shapes and not to specific varieties of plants.

Thus Sullivan did not simply take a single plant and reduce it to an abstract representation as, for example, the ancient Egyptians did with the Papyrus and Lotus. He sought instead to compose his ornament out of various botanical shapes according to principles of design discovered by studying botany. That Sullivan studied plants and flowers morphologically, not with the aim of turning individual plants into ornaments but in order to learn nature's principles of composition, is also implied by his rigorously scientific drawing of a dissected Lotus (Fig. 12).[9]

From the evidence of Sullivan's early fresco drawings it is thus possible to trace his ornament visually to the work of Victorian architects and intellectually to the search for principles of design in plants and flowers. Out of these sources and principles Sullivan evolved his system of ornament.

STYLE AND TECHNIQUE. Sullivan's drawings for ornament constitute the bulk of his preserved graphic work. Those at the Avery Library illustrate all the chronological stylistic periods into which his ornament can be divided. The drawings also illustrate the changes in Sullivan's drawing technique that roughly paralleled the stylistic evolution of his ornament.

Sullivan's earliest ornamental period is known to us only through his drawings. Preserved from the mid 1870's are a number of pen-and-ink tracings (Nos. 2-8) made from pencil drawings, all apparently intended for interior decorations of Chicago buildings.[10]

[7] Pugin as writer is perhaps best-known for his *True Principles of Christian or Pointed Architecture*, 1841, and Jones, for his *Grammar of Ornament*, 1856. For Pugin see Phoebe Stanton, *Pugin* (New York, 1972). Owen Jones does not yet have a biographer.

[8] Louis Sullivan, *A System of Architectural Ornament*, pls. 2, 5.

[9] "Lotos Club Notebook," p. 161, Avery Library, Columbia University. Although purchased for taking notes in the architectural lectures at M.I.T., the book was mainly used as a sketchbook by Sullivan and his friends at the Lotos Club on the Calumet River at Riverdale, Illinois, see Sullivan, *Autobiography*, pp. 210-11, and Connely, *Louis Sullivan as He Lived*, pp. 69-79.

[10] It is known that Sullivan prepared fresco decorations for two buildings in Chicago. The first was the Moody Church on Chicago Avenue designed by Sullivan's friend John Edelmann. The second, Sinai Temple, was the work of Dankmar Adler, who would later become Sullivan's partner. As the frescoes in both buildings were not carried out until 1876, it is not possible to associate them with any

These pen-and-ink drawings are composed of conventionalized leaves, stems, and flowers executed in a two-dimensional linear technique without illusionistic shading. In one of them there is also a schematized bird. Whether or not Sullivan produced stylistically similar three-dimensional designs cannot be answered, for as yet no one has discovered any architectural ornaments or drawings for such ornament dating from the mid 1870's.

The only pencil drawings (Figs. 8-10) that survive for these pen-and-ink tracings are characterized by fine, carefully controlled lines of uniform thickness.[11] The few hatched areas are equally precise, add only contrast, and do not contribute any illusion of depth.

Sullivan's ornament during the 1880's may be divided into three phases. The first, lasting from 1879 to 1883, is illustrated in the Avery collection by a drawing of 1882 for the porch capitals of Marx Wineman's house in Chicago (No. 12).[12] During these years, Sullivan carefully separated his ornamental motifs from each other by avoiding interpenetrating parts and by placing each motif against a smooth ground plane. His sharply delineated botanical abstractions consisted of fan-shaped leaves and petals, spiral leaves with scalloped edges, broad leaves resembling scallop shells, and smooth-edged leaves. The last type appears in two versions in the Wineman drawing. The one is shaped like an ordinary petal and the other like an arrowhead with only one barb.

In 1883 Sullivan's ornament became more complex. A drawing in the Avery collection for the remodeling of the McVicker's Theater (No. 14) illustrates this phase, which lasted until 1885. During this period motifs were intertwined and overlapped, integrating the ornament in both two and three dimensions. To this end the former individuality of each motif was sacrificed. A freer, more vivacious curvilinear rhythm began to manifest itself. New motifs such as elongated buds and sinuous tendrils also appeared.

From 1885 through 1889 Sullivan's ornament lost much of its former angularity and became more sophisticated and luxuriant (Nos. 15-31). Compositions were more relaxed and linear elements more flowing than in his ornament before 1885. Botanical motifs were freed from the previous restrictive schematization and became more natural although not entirely naturalistic. A prominent new motif that appeared was a leaf whose flaccid surface was presented frontally. During these years Sullivan's ornament is especially marked by the sharply pointed lobes of his leaves and flowers.

In the 1880's Sullivan's graphic technique, like his ornament, gradually became freer and more vibrant. Although Sullivan now employed illusionistic shading to suggest the degree of relief in his plastic ornaments, he also used shading graphically, as a foil for the fine lines with which he constructed his motifs. Where the lines in his drawings of the 1870's were well-defined, of uniform width, and delineated with precision, his later lines gradually became more varied in tone and acquired an increasing sense of lyrical movement.

In 1890 Sullivan's ornament reached maturity. Beginning with his designs of that year for ornamentation in the Auditorium Banquet Hall (Nos. 32-34) and continuing

---

of the drawings in the Avery collection. For a discussion of these frescoes see Connely, *Louis Sullivan as He Lived*, pp. 80-85.

[11] In the Emil Lorch Papers at the Michigan Historical Collections of the Bentley Historical Library, the University of Michigan, Ann Arbor.

[12] Wineman's first name is consistently spelled "Marx" in the Chicago city directories.

throughout the decade of the 1890's (Nos. 35-114), Sullivan attained the summit of elegance and sophistication in his designs for ornament. During these years Sullivan also eliminated from his ornament nearly all specific vestiges of his American and European antecedents so that his ornament thus truly became modern. His earlier pointed leaves gave way to ones that were rounded and succulent while his smooth ground plane was replaced by textured patterns.

An equally abrupt change in Sullivan's graphic technique coincided with the appearance of his mature ornament. His studies for the carved-wood capitals of the Auditorium Banquet Hall, dating from April through July 1890 (Nos. 32-34), were no longer constructed of lines and shadows in the conventional sense but of broken lines and dots whose character was determined by subtle variations both in the angle and pressure applied to the pencil. Although it is unlikely that this light-dark technique was suggested by European Impressionism, the effects are similar. If this manner was indeed stimulated by some contemporary art, the more likely source is H. H. Richardson's Byzantinesque ornament of 1880-1886.

From 1892 to 1894 geometrical patterns dominate Sullivan's ornament, almost completely replacing organic forms (Nos. 57-86). Sullivan restricted the latter to leafy passages added here and there for contrast. His decorations of these years are also characterized by an emphasis on the upper or forward surface of the ornament. He achieved this effect by sinking the negative areas of these geometric designs into or beneath that surface. Sullivan thus reversed his previous method of composing outward from the background plane.

In 1894 Sullivan combined new, relatively large shield-shaped devices having plain surfaces with his geometric ornament. The most common shapes were triangular with the point down and rectangular with inward curvature on the sides. During this period (Nos. 87-115), lasting from 1895 to about 1902, Sullivan also made considerable use of curling branches usually having broad surfaces punctuated by leafy passages. He continued to employ the sinuous geometry of his previous period but now he used it as a background against which the more fluent shield-shaped and organic motifs were seen.

Sullivan's style of drawing during the decade of the 1890's remained so uniform that it is not possible to distinguish in his graphic work the three stylistic phases that mark his ornament of that period. In most of his drawings there is a mingling of his light-dark manner—usually shaded to some degree—and an uninhibited and vivacious linear style. What variations there are in Sullivan's graphic technique during these years may be explained by changes in his ornamental style or by the differing uses of the drawings.[13]

By 1910, when Sullivan designed the cover for *Gibson's Magazine* (No. 122), he had evolved the style which continued until his death in 1924. Certain characteristics of

[13] In *Genius and the Mobocracy*, Wright compares a drawing of 1890 for McVicker's Theater (No. 40) with another of 1895 for the Guaranty Building (No. 96) and discerns a change in Sullivan's technique of drawing between those years. But what Wright did was to compare two quite different kinds of drawings; the earlier (No. 40) is a very free ornamental sketch and the later (No. 96) a more restrained working drawing. Had he compared either sketches or working drawings, differences in rendering not related to changes in Sullivan's ornamental style would certainly have been much less obvious. Why Wright, who served as Sullivan's chief draftsman from 1888 to 1893, would have made such an inappropriate comparison is difficult to understand.

Sullivan's late work—such as the clustering of leaves at the ends of long, sagging branches —are evident in his design for the cover. The broad unopened bud atop the vertical stalk is also often encountered in Sullivan's late ornament.

Another drawing in a different collection at Avery, made in 1920 for a proposed remodeling of Sullivan's Land and Loan Office at Algona, Iowa (Fig. 61), illustrates other aspects of Sullivan's final ornamental period. Its branches overlap in such a way that they cancel their own directions of movement. Its other motifs are carefully separated from each other. The result is a diminishing of the rhythmical interaction of lines and shapes so characteristic of Sullivan's early ornament. In these late drawings the minutiae of dots and broken lines of Sullivan's mature period is largely replaced by areas of solid and hatched shadows that suggest both depth and plasticity.

OFFICE PROCEDURE. To interpret Sullivan's ornamental drawings, it is necessary to know something about the various kinds of drawings in the Avery collection and the probable uses of each. It is likely that as many as four different types of drawings for each ornamental design were produced by Sullivan's office: a summary sketch at small scale, a more detailed sketch at larger scale, a working drawing to a fixed scale, and a full-size working drawing. As no design in the Avery collection is carried through more than two of these steps, it is impossible to prove that any ornament was worked up through all stages.

The Avery drawings are executed on four different kinds of stock and it would appear that the choice of paper was partly conditioned by the stage of design. Thus ordinary paper, including Adler & Sullivan stationery, was generally selected by Sullivan for the initial sketches. For working drawings he and his staff used either a medium- or a heavy-weight drawing paper. Tracing paper seems to have been used only at the working drawing stage, primarily for compositional purposes. Although many of the drawings were eventually traced onto linen, there is only one drawing of that kind for an unexecuted pair of ornamental gates among the Avery drawings (No. 56).

There are a number of designs carried through the two-sketch sequence in the Avery collection. The ground floor capitals of the Guaranty Building were initially set down in an apparently hurried fashion on office stationery (No. 98). Two days later Sullivan worked the capital out in greater detail (No. 99). His label "Finis" on the second sketch implies that his personal part in making the design was finished. Working drawings for the capital, which were most certainly needed because his sketches only show the capital in perspective, were thus to be made by someone else, most likely Sullivan's chief draftsman.

Sullivan's drawings for an oratory medal follow the same pattern. The first, made January 29, 1895, shows both sides of the medal on a single sheet of paper (No. 90). The second, dated the next day and illustrating only the reverse of the medal, is worked out in much greater detail at twice the intended scale (No. 91). No doubt Sullivan also redrew the obverse of the medal, but no drawing for it is known.

Twenty-six drawings in the Avery collection appear to be either scale or full-size working drawings or tracings made from such drawings.[14] Three scales were employed.

[14] Nos. 4-8, 12, 26, 31, 33-34, 37, 39, 41, 53-54, 56, 61, 65, 96, 113-114, 116-117, 119-120, 121.

The most common is one and one-half inches to the foot. Representative examples of working drawings in the Avery collection are the one for a corbel in the Auditorium Building (No. 26), for a capital in the Auditorium Banquet Hall (No. 34), for a stair railing angle block in the Chicago Stock Exchange Building (No. 61), and for a pier in the Guaranty Building at Buffalo (No. 96).

Of these twenty-six working drawings, Sullivan personally made seventeen of them: fifteen to scale (Nos. 4-8, 26, 33-34, 37, 41, 53, 65, 96, 113-14) and two full size (Nos. 12, 61). Why he bothered to make working drawings is a question that cannot be answered with certainty. No doubt during the early 1880's when Adler & Sullivan had relatively few commissions and a small staff, Sullivan had necessarily to enlarge most of his sketches into working drawings. But this situation presumably changed dramatically in 1888 when, faced with the tremendous increase in work occasioned by the Auditorium commission, Sullivan had to look for a special assistant, whom he found in the person of Frank Lloyd Wright, to help him convert his ornamental sketches into scale drawings. Even then, as the Avery collection testifies, Sullivan never entirely gave up making working drawings himself. The reason he continued to do so is suggested by the drawings themselves, nearly all of which were made during periods when the firm was extremely busy. Sullivan even drew one of them, for the balcony front of McVicker's Theater (No. 41), on Christmas Day, 1890. Presumably at times like that Sullivan had no choice but to assist in the preparation of working drawings. It may also be that those designs which carried a special interest for Sullivan received his personal attention from summary sketch through working drawings.

About thirty of the ornamental designs in the Avery collection correspond to ornaments that may be studied *in situ*, in collections of ornament, or in photographs, thus permitting comparisons between ornaments as drawn and executed. Predictably the correspondence between design and execution increases as one goes from the initial to the developed sketch and from that sketch to scale and full-size working drawings. Taking Sullivan's drawings for the Guaranty Building as an example, we find that his initial sketches survive for a terra-cotta capital (No. 98; Fig. 46), a cast-iron escutcheon plate (No. 97; Fig. 45) and a cast-iron baluster (No. 94; Fig. 43). In each case it is obvious that these summary sketches must have been further developed in drawings now lost before the plaster models were made. Even Sullivan's fully developed sketch labeled "Finis" for the Guaranty capital (No. 99; Fig. 46) lacks sufficient detail for even the most thoroughly sympathetic sculptor to have used as a model. The same is true for a working drawing personally made by Sullivan for an interior column (No. 96; Fig. 44). Although in its details the executed column is very close to Sullivan's relatively precise elevation of the column face, it is obvious that numerous changes of detail and proportion were made during the modeling process. The same even applies to the few full-size drawings in the collection where a comparison is possible. For example, when the drawing for the front of the Getty Tomb (No. 39) is compared with its carved surface (Fig. 27), it is easy to detect many changes of detail evidently introduced by the stone carver.

Yet, in spite of the many changes and additions to the details of Sullivan's sketches as they were worked up by his chief draftsman and converted into ornament by his modeler or carver, the final result rarely departs in any essential from the spirit of the original design. This indicates that although Sullivan probably did not often make working

9

drawings for his ornament, and surely never modeled any of it, he must have closely supervised his chief assistants. That he took great care in their selection and training—and this includes the craftsmen who carved and modeled his ornament—is also obvious from the high caliber of the persons who served Sullivan. The first of his chief draftsmen was Frank Lloyd Wright, who worked for him from 1888 to 1893, then came George Elmslie, 1893 to 1909,[15] and finally Parker Berry, 1909 to 1917.[16] Almost all of Sullivan's cast ornament from the Auditorium Building on was modeled by Kristian Schneider, an artist-craftsman whom Sullivan had personally trained to execute his designs.[17]

Comparisons between Sullivan's drawings and the ornaments made from them also provide abundant evidence that in making his sketches Sullivan paid little attention to the nature of the intended material or the position of the ornament on a building. Sullivan's sketches, mostly on paper of letter size or smaller, all contain about the same amount of detail regardless of the intended final size or material. Thus there is hardly any difference in the clarity of ornamental details between Sullivan's drawing for a circular plaster panel of five-foot diameter in McVicker's Theater (No. 42; cf. Fig. 29), and his studies for a bronze medal with a diameter of two and one-half inches (Nos. 90-91; Figs. 41-42), or between Sullivan's sketch for a three-foot high cast-iron baluster in the Guaranty Building (No. 94; Fig. 43) and another sketch for a cast-iron escutcheon plate in the same building less than one foot high (No. 97; Fig. 45).

As executed, Sullivan's ornament followed traditional usage. The closer it was to the observer, the finer its detail and the smaller its scale. Materials such as cast-iron and cast-bronze capable of reproducing finely detailed designs were ornamented with intricate patterns. Materials such as terra cotta were impressed with designs of greater breadth and coarseness. In practice Sullivan tried to use materials capable of receiving fine detail in positions close to the observer and those requiring designs of a coarser kind at greater distances.

That Sullivan's executed ornament should thus vary according to the material used and its position on the building, while his sketches for the same ornaments remained technically and stylistically very similar, indicates that Sullivan preferred to wait at least until working drawings before adjusting his ornamental designs to the realities of scale and material. This means that except for those few working drawings personally made by Sullivan this task was entrusted—no doubt under Sullivan's close supervision—to his carefully selected and trained assistants.

ARCHITECTURAL DRAWINGS

Compared with Sullivan's many studies for ornament, only a small fraction of his drawings for buildings has survived. Yet among these few, there is sufficient variety to enable

[15] George Grant Elmslie (1871-1952) emigrated from Scotland in 1884 and entered the architectural office of Joseph Silsbee in 1887. In 1890 he joined Adler & Sullivan and in 1893, when Wright left the office, he became chief draftsman under Sullivan. This arrangement continued until 1909 when Elmslie left Sullivan to enter private practice with William Purcell and George Feick. For Elmslie, see H. Allen Brooks, *The Prairie School* (Toronto, 1972).

[16] Parker N. Berry (1888-1918) worked for Sullivan from 1909 until 1917 when he entered private practice. Berry's work is the subject of an article by Donald Hoffmann, "The Brief Career of a Sullivan Apprentice: Parker N. Berry," *The Prairie School Review*, IV (Fourth Quarter, 1967), 7-15.

[17] Morrison, *Louis Sullivan*, pp. 200-201.

the observer to draw certain conclusions about Sullivan's method of designing buildings. For that purpose, however, it is helpful to supplement the three architectural sketches in the Avery collection (Nos. 13, 79, 106) with two others made by Sullivan in 1913 for the Merchants' National Bank at Grinnell, Iowa (Figs. 54, 56).[18]

Because of their impromptu technique and the paper used, it is evident that all of these drawings represent a very early stage in Sullivan's process of architectural design. In this sense, these drawings are the architectural equivalents of Sullivan's sketches for ornament. His elevation of a tall building drawn in 1894 was made on a piece of office stationery (No. 79). For the country club of 1898 (No. 106) he used the back of one of his business cards. His perspective study of 1883 for boxes in McVicker's Theater (No. 13) is equally spontaneous even though executed on a conventional sheet of drawing paper. His drawings for the Grinnell bank were made on ordinary letterhead stationery obtained from the Storm Pharmacy in Grinnell (Figs. 54, 56).

Sullivan's method of working up his architectural designs from freehand sketches was very likely a reflection of his training at the École des Beaux-Arts in Paris. His evident haste in wanting to set down the architectural vision before it became blurred even in the slightest degree presumably derives from the method at the French school of working from, and staying as close as possible to, the *esquisse*. This meant that after carefully reviewing the program of requirements, each student made a sketch of his solution in terms of plan, section, and elevation and filed a copy with the school. Although he might thereafter spend considerable time elaborating these sketches and working out their details, the theory of the school required that he retain the essentials of the original scheme. About this method Sullivan later wrote in his autobiography, "Louis thought the exigent condition that one hold to the original sketch in its essentials, to be a discipline, of an inspired sort, in that it held one firmly to a thesis."[19] That Sullivan thought of the Grinnell drawings as an *esquisse* seems evident from only a glance at the finished building (Fig. 55) which hardly departs in any respect from Sullivan's studies—a plan and two elevations—made over a three-day period from November 28 to 30, 1913.

Sullivan also seems to have embraced the idea of holding to an *esquisse* when designing architectural ornament. A comparison of Sullivan's sketchy indications for ornament on his preliminary elevations for the Grinnell bank and the ornament of the building as finished (Figs. 54-56) reveals a remarkable similarity between conception and execution. Although Sullivan may have returned to the ornament of his initial elevations when, many months later, he began working out the details of the ornament, it is more likely he followed a somewhat different procedure based on the theory of the *esquisse*. It is described for us by George Elmslie, who, in speaking of his independent practice after leaving Sullivan, writes: "While the design of the building is being worked out thumb-nail motifs for the decorations are also being worked out and filed away so as to preserve the original impulse."[20] The next step was certainly to retrieve the thumbnail sketches as progress on the commission demanded and to make from them larger but still sketchy ornamental studies. Although it can hardly be doubted that Elmslie learned

---

[18] These two drawings, and one other showing a side elevation of the bank, are among the Emil Lorch Papers in the Michigan Historical Collections of the Bentley Historical Library, the University of Michigan, Ann Arbor.

[19] Sullivan, *Autobiography*, p. 238.

[20] "The Statics and Dynamics of Architecture," *Western Architect*, XIX (January 1913), 24.

this method of design from Sullivan, the absence of thumbnail sketches in the Avery and other collections makes it impossible to prove that Sullivan actually worked in this manner.

The Grinnell drawings also call attention to another theoretical principle which Sullivan absorbed while at the École des Beaux-Arts and which he seems to have made an integral part of his own method. Of the studies Sullivan prepared while at Grinnell, the first in date was the plan. That Sullivan was fully cognizant of this especially important aspect of French architectural theory is clear from the passage in his autobiography where he writes that he "familiarized himself thoroughly with the theory of the School, which, in his mind, settled down to a theory of *plan*, yielding results of extraordinary brilliancy, but which, after all, was not the reality he sought, but an abstraction, a method, a state of mind, that was local and specific; not universal."[21] Although this somewhat negative statement might suggest that Sullivan did not in practice follow the school's theory of plan, the Grinnell drawings suggest that in fact he did. His letter to Claude Bragdon written in 1904 also implies as much, "I believe I *absorbed* the real principles that the school *envelops*, so to speak—my work has consistently shown this."[22]

In embracing the French theories of plan and *esquisse*, Sullivan remained firmly wedded to his time and place. To hold strictly to the *esquisse* meant that Sullivan denied himself the kind of experimentation that could have resulted in new ways of visualizing architectural space, massing, sequence, and the like. By insisting upon the preeminence of plan, he could hardly have begun to imagine buildings with the spatial complexity of a Wright or a Le Corbusier.

An almost mystical aspect of Sullivan's architectural vision is especially noticeable in a group of architectural drawings for the Farmers' and Merchants' Union Bank of 1919 at Columbus, Wisconsin (Figs. 57-58), preserved at the Avery Library.[23] At each stage in revising this design, Sullivan worked freehand in pencil, as though struggling to stay abreast of the flow of ideas. Even in a section through the building (Fig. 58) dated several months after the first studies—and at this point very nearly a working drawing— Sullivan continued to draw freehand. Only a few horizontal and vertical lines, and the semicircular frames of the windows, seem the product of drawing instruments; all the rest, complete with dimensions, lettering, and other details, testifies to Sullivan's deft manipulation of the freehand pencil. In the hands of so skilled a draftsman, even mundane architectural drawings such as plans and sections become exceptional works of graphic art.

Although it cannot be proven absolutely, because so few architectural drawings remain, the easy unfettered quality of the Columbus drawings imply that, in making them, Sullivan was working in a manner to which he had long been accustomed. If this was Sullivan's usual method, he must ordinarily have shunned drawing instruments and instead worked up his architectural drawings freehand until they were ready for a draftsman to convert into working drawings. But whatever the exact case, Sullivan's drawings for the banks at Grinnell and Columbus together with the architectural drawings in the

---

[21] Sullivan, *Autobiography*, p. 240.
[22] Claude Bragdon, "Letters from Louis Sullivan," *Architecture*, LXIV (July 1931), 8.

[23] Nine of these drawings were published as part of a reprinting in 1967 of Sullivan's *A System of Architectural Ornament*.

12

Avery collection augment the testimony of Sullivan's ornamental drawings concerning his brilliance as graphic artist. The tragedy, of course, is that so little of this part of Sullivan's work survives.

FIGURE DRAWINGS

Other kinds of drawings by Sullivan are preserved in several collections. They include caricatures, cartoons, grotesques, portraits, nude figures, and anatomical and botanical studies. Only one of these subjects, the nude figure, is represented in the Avery collection.[24] The three drawings at Avery (Nos. 9-11) belong to a series of twenty-two similar drawings of nude figures that Sullivan began December 26, 1877, and concluded August 30, 1885. Although Sullivan may have made some of these drawings from live models, it is more likely that he copied or traced most of them from textbooks on drawing the human figure.[25]

Semi-nude figures were eventually to find their way into Sullivan's architecture in the form of decorative figure sculpture and painting. Sullivan's best-known buildings in which such figures played a significant part in the decorative scheme were the Transportation Building of 1891-1893 at the Columbian Exposition in Chicago and the Bayard Building of 1897-1898 in New York City.[26] A large tracing in the Avery collection shows the abstract winged-figures that were painted on the facades of the Transportation Building (No. 54). Also in the collection is a working drawing for the ornamental fountains that projected from the main front of the exposition building (No. 53). Incorporated into its ornamental details are nude figures that closely resemble the ones in Sullivan's drawings of 1877-1880 (Nos. 9-11). A sketch by Sullivan for an ornamental detail of the famous entrance arch to the Transportation Building also contains a nude figure (No. 52). In this case, Sullivan's source may have been an Italian Renaissance putto. Finally, for the title page of a projected reprinting of his poem "Inspiration"[27] Sullivan apparently made a tracing that combines lettering, ornament, and a nude figure (No. 93).

CONCLUSION

Frank Lloyd Wright's personal tribute to Sullivan, published in 1949 and called *Genius and the Mobocracy*, contains illustrations of thirty-nine of the drawings in the Avery collection. In making selections for the book Wright correctly emphasized Sullivan's ornamental sketches, which so intimately document Sullivan's talents as designer and draftsman. No doubt Wright included four of the early fresco tracings and four scale and two full-size working drawings, even though one of the latter two are not by Sullivan,

---

[24] Three are in the Avery collection (Nos. 9-11), one is among the Lorch papers in the Michigan Historical Collections, and the rest are in the Sullivan collection at the Burnham Library of The Art Institute of Chicago.

[25] See Nos. 9-11.

[26] For illustrations of these buildings see Morrison, *Louis Sullivan*, figs. 44-45, 58.

[27] Sullivan wrote "Inspiration" in 1886. After presenting it in that year before the annual convention of the Western Society of Architects, he had the poem published by the Inland Architect Press.

in order to provide examples from all periods of Sullivan's work and to show the various stages through which designs progressed in the Adler & Sullivan office. Less easy to understand is why Wright failed to include any of the exquisite studies for stencils in the St. Nicholas Hotel at St. Louis or, with the single exception of a lady's comb, any of Sullivan's sketches for small objects and covers. Perhaps Wright felt that designs of this character, however elegant, did not enhance Sullivan's stature as architect.

While it is thus difficult to fault Wright's selection of the drawings that illustrate *Genius and the Mobocracy*, one searches almost vainly for a reason to justify Wright's insensitive treatment of the Avery drawings when preparing them for publication. Why, if Wright really believed the drawings "poignantly beautiful rhythms,"[28] did he mark them up with crop lines and editorial scribbles? Perhaps he really regarded the drawings only as means to the ends of architecture and ornament and of little value in themselves. Was publication of the drawings only an inconvenient necessity arising out of his promise to the dying Sullivan to write about them,[29] a promise to be fulfilled by Wright in the most expeditious manner possible? Certainly the rough treatment Wright gave the drawings suggests as much and implies that he believed publication of the drawings more important than the drawings themselves.

The drawings that appear in *Genius and the Mobocracy* together with the others in the Avery collection represent only a small fraction of those that must have been prepared by Sullivan and his staff for architectural and ornamental projects. Why so few of these drawings are preserved is an intriguing question. If, as Wright reports, Sullivan considered these drawings "the dearest treasure of his heart,"[30] why did he keep so few of them? And why, when retaining so small a percentage of the drawings prepared during a fifty-year career, did Sullivan choose to preserve scale and full-size working drawings executed by his draftsmen? Why also is it that the drawings do not cover the range and time span of Sullivan's work in a more comprehensive manner?

It is not sufficient to lay blame for the loss of Sullivan's drawings on the tidy habits of George Elmslie, Sullivan's chief draftsman from 1893 to 1909, as Willard Connely does in his *Louis Sullivan as He Lived*.[31] If Elmslie was to blame, why do so many of the Avery drawings date from the period when Elmslie was chief draftsman? Nor does it explain why no drawings survive for architectural ornament from the decade after Elmslie left Sullivan's employ. There are not even any ornamental drawings preserved for Sullivan's bank at Columbus, Wisconsin, of 1919, or for the facade of the Krause Music Store of 1922, both of which were carried out by Sullivan with little or no assistance.

These facts seem to lead to the conclusion that the drawings in the Avery collection are the unplanned, accidental, and random survivors of fifty years of graphic work by Louis Sullivan and his staff. The truth appears to be that Sullivan looked upon his architectural and ornamental drawings, whether sketches or scale drawings, as utilitarian documents without special value in and of themselves, to be discarded when the goal of constructing an artistic building was attained. Had Sullivan regarded his sketches as we regard them today, that is, as independent works of art, and his working drawings as important

[28] Frank Lloyd Wright, *Genius and the Mobocracy*, p. 58.

[29] *Ibid.*, pp. 74, 101.   [30] *Ibid.*, p. 101.

[31] Connely, *Louis Sullivan as He Lived*, p. 236.

14

historical documents, he would certainly have taken a much greater interest in preserving them. But he did not and they were thrown away, first by Sullivan himself, and later by each of his chief draftsmen. The result of this misconception, surely one of the great tragedies in the history of architecture, is that of the literally thousands of pencil sketches prepared by Louis Sullivan for his buildings and ornament, fewer than two hundred survive today. But what survives almost miraculously or what Sullivan kept in spite of everything, is of exquisite quality, as the following pages will demonstrate.

THE CATALOGUE

A NOTE TO THE READER

Whenever possible, the drawings are arranged chronologically and if feasible they are presented in groups, organized either by style and technique or according to the project for which they were intended. For those drawings that appear under a single heading, the comment is reserved where possible for the group as a whole.

Several entries commonly included in catalogues of this type will not be found. Because the drawings passed directly from Sullivan to Wright, and later from the Taliesin Foundation to the Avery Library, there is no provenance entry. Also, as there has not been any scholarly comment on the drawings, the usual entry for literature is not given.

Since the few drawings that have been reproduced have appeared without comment, the customary entry referring to previous reproduction is not needed. Instead, the abbreviation "*Genius*" is employed to identify these drawings reproduced by Frank Lloyd Wright in his important book entitled *Genius and the Mobocracy*, which deals with Sullivan and his drawings. Although Wright never commented in his text on individual drawings, he nevertheless made significant judgments about them in selecting those that illustrate his book and in wording the captions that accompany them. It is also of interest to know which drawings Wright published in *Genius* because he annotated those drawings with the editorial remarks and notations that still mar them today.

FORMAT. The first line in each entry includes the Catalogue number (referred to as "No." in the text); the subject and date; the number of a comparative illustration when included (referred to as "Fig." in the text); and the number assigned the drawing by the Taliesin Foundation. The original inscriptions and annotations follow in italics. Since all of the drawings are illustrated, dimensions by Sullivan are not always quoted and the inscriptions have not been divided to show the line breaks.

Medium, character of paper (if significant), and dimensions (in inches and centimeters) follow. The measurements have been taken at the longest vertical and horizontal dimension of each drawing, the height preceding the width. Unless otherwise noted, all unsigned drawings are attributed to Sullivan by drawing style and handwriting. The last entry reproduces in italics Wright's caption for the drawing as it appears in *Genius*.

The Burnham Library of the Art Institute of Chicago and the Emil Lorch papers in the Michigan Historical Collections of the Bentley Historical Library at the University of Michigan, Ann Arbor, Michigan, are referred to respectively as the Burnham Library and the Lorch Papers.

CATALOGUE CONTENTS

THE CATALOGUE

STUDENT WORK [?]

1. STUDY OF A FLAME, about 1872. FLLW/LHS No. 114

Legend in pencil: *Form & Sizes of flames from a 5-foot fish tail, bare-tip burner. (F's Circ)*. The drawing is also annotated as follows: in the flames: *5 feet per hour, 4 feet " ", 3 " " ", 2 " " ", 1 foot per hour*; and in the lower left-hand corner: *10-14-78* [?].
Pencil.
7 1/8 x 4 in. 18.1 x 10.2 cm.

Although the final notation seems to be a date, it is difficult to imagine why Sullivan would have made a drawing of this type in 1878. It is more likely that he made it between 1870 and 1872 as a student exercise, possibly for a physics class, while studying at the English High School in Boston. Fish-tail burners were used in laboratories until about a generation ago to produce a flat, fan-shaped flame for bending and joining glass apparatus. The drawing seems to show the effects of various gas pressures expressed in feet-per-hour on the size and shape of the flame. If the drawing was made as a secondary school project, we must then suppose that the notation in question refers to something other than the date of execution.

FRESCO DESIGNS

2. FRESCO DESIGN [?], dated 1873. FLLW/LHS No. 93

Inscribed in pencil: *First Effort 1873.*
Purple ink on tracing paper.
8 1/4 x 7 1/2 in. 21.0 x 19.0 cm.

3. FRESCO DESIGN [?], dated 1873. FLLW/LHS No. 11

Inscribed in pencil: *First Effort 1873.*
Purple ink on tracing paper.
6 3/4 x 6 1/2 in. 17.2 x 16.5 cm.

4. FRESCO DESIGN, dated Nov. 29, 1874. (Figs. 8-9) FLLW/LHS No. 18

Legend in ink: *Fresco-Border on ceiling. To correspond with Center-piece and Frieze. Louis H. Sullivan to John H. Edelmann. Paris, Nov. 29th 1874.* Annotations in pencil by Frank Lloyd Wright at lower right: *In . . . Space, cut*, and associated crop marks.
Purple ink on tracing paper.
10 1/2 x 16 5/16 in. 26.5 x 41.3 cm.
Genius, with caption: *Dedicated to John Edelman [sic]. Early exercise at the Beaux Arts. Paris. 1875-80* (only right-half of drawing is illustrated).

23

5. FRESCO DESIGN, dated Apr. 1, 1875.   (Fig. 10)   FLLW/LHS No. 33

Legend in ink: *Center-piece in Fresco. Louis H. Sullivan to John H. Edelman [sic].*
Paris. April 1st 1875. Annotations in pencil by Frank Lloyd Wright in upper left corner: *cut*, and associated crop marks.
Ink on tracing paper.
19 3/4 x 16 3/8 in.   50.0 x 41.5 cm.
Genius, with caption: *Beaux Arts exercises. Fresco patterns. Paris. 1875.*

6. FRESCO DESIGN, dated Apr. 1, 1875.   (Fig. 10)   FLLW/LHS No. 17

Legend in ink: *Fresco-border. Louis H. Sullivan to John H. Edelman [sic]. Paris.*
April 1st 1875.
Ink on tracing paper.
10 3/8 x 16 5/16 in.   26.3 x 41.3 cm.
A few details of the center plant are in pencil.

7. FRESCO DESIGN, dated July 11, 1875.   FLLW/LHS No. 32

Legend in ink: *Center-piece in Fresco. Louis H. Sullivan, July 11th 1875.* Annotations in pencil by Frank Lloyd Wright at the bottom left: *cut, #4, Reduce to 3 1/4"*;
in the upper right corner: *cut,* and associated crop marks.
Ink on tracing paper.
20 1/4 x 16 5/16 in.   51.2 x 41.3 cm.
Genius, with caption: *Beaux Arts exercises. Fresco patterns. Paris. 1875.*

8. FRESCO DESIGN, dated July 11, 1875.   FLLW/LHS No. 19

Legend in ink: *Border in Fresco. Louis H. Sullivan, July 11th, 1875.* Annotations in pencil by Frank Lloyd Wright at bottom and top: *cut, reduce to 4 3/8"*, and associated crop marks.
Ink on tracing paper.
10 3/8 x 16 5/16 in.   26.3 x 41.3 cm.
Genius, with caption: *Beaux Arts exercises. Fresco patterns. Paris. 1875.*

According to their inscriptions, drawings Nos. 4-8, dated 1874-1875, were made as models for ornamental frescoes. The two other drawings (Nos. 2-3), dated 1873, may have been made for the same purpose as they are closely related to Nos. 4-8 in style, technique, and paper. If they were, it is also likely that all of these drawings were made by Sullivan for the interior decoration of buildings designed by Sullivan's close friend in Chicago, the architect John Edelmann.[1] Such a conclusion is suggested not only because Edelmann's name appears on the three drawings made in Paris but also because Sullivan

---

[1] Sullivan met John Edelmann (1852-1900) late in 1873 in the architectural office of William Le Baron Jenney in Chicago where Edelmann was foreman. Between 1874 and 1876 Edelmann associated himself with Joseph S. Johnston in an architectural partnership. In 1876 Edelmann left for Cleveland but on his return to Chicago around 1879 he renewed his close friendship with Sullivan and maintained it for the two years he stayed there. Sullivan sometimes dropped the final "n" in Edelmann's name. See further on Edelmann in Donald D. Egbert and Paul Sprague, "In Search of John Edelmann," *Journal of the American Institute of Architects*, XLV (February 1966), 35-41; and Louis Sullivan, *The Autobiography of an Idea* (New York, 1924; repr. 1956).

later prepared the fresco decorations for Moody's Church in Chicago, a building designed by Edelmann's firm of Johnston & Edelmann.[2] As the frescoing of Moody's Church was not carried out until 1876, it is impossible to associate any of the drawings in this group with that commission. For the same reason—incompatible dates—none of these drawings can be related to Sullivan's other recorded early decorative commission in Chicago, the frescoing in 1876 of Sinai Temple.[3] The Sinai commission probably came to Sullivan through Edelmann who formerly had worked for its architect, Dankmar Adler, later to become Sullivan's partner.

Except for these documented connections between Sullivan and Edelmann, one might well suppose that the two earliest drawings dated 1873 (Nos. 2-3) were made while Sullivan was working in Philadelphia for Frank Furness. Certainly Sullivan's arrival in Chicago on the day before Thanksgiving, 1873,[4] would have left little time for Sullivan to have come to know Edelmann well enough to be designing frescoes for him before the end of the year. If, however, we suppose the dates on the drawings are incorrect and that Sullivan actually made them in 1874, the difficulty of associating the drawings with Edelmann disappears.

That the dates may not be correct is suggested by the inscriptions on the drawings, which seem to be additions. They are in pencil while the drawings are in ink and they are worded as if to indicate hindsight: "First Effort, 1873." Certainly it is unlikely that when making these drawings Sullivan knew they were to be the first efforts in a series that would extend over a number of years. Had Sullivan added these inscriptions after a lapse of many years, perhaps even decades, he might easily have forgotten the exact year in which he made them. Perhaps it was to these very drawings that Frank Lloyd Wright referred when, in *Genius*, he wrote that before Sullivan gave him the drawings, Sullivan "had been dating the drawings (some wrongly but who really knows?). . . ."[5] If these two early drawings were not made in 1873, the most likely time would have been between January and July 1874, while Sullivan was working in Chicago but before he set out for Paris and the École des Beaux-Arts.

It is interesting that even while a student in Paris Sullivan was designing frescoes for Edelmann. Wright assumed that the three drawings (Nos. 4-6), which are signed Paris and are inscribed "to John Edelman [*sic*]," were student exercises at the École des Beaux-Arts. Willard Connely, in a later expansion of Wright's assumption, wrote about No. 4 that "Part of Louis' 'project' for Vaudremer, now, was to decorate a room. By late November, the 29th, the pupil had arrived at the ceiling of it."[6] Yet, for several reasons, it is unlikely that either Wright or Connely are correct. Beaux-Arts *projects* rarely included interior designing and, even if Sullivan had been assigned such a *project*, it is highly improbable that an assignment of that kind would have been followed by another of a similar character less than half a year later; yet that is what the two drawings (Nos. 5-6) of April 1, 1875, otherwise imply. Nor does it seem reasonable that Sullivan would have sent the drawings to Edelmann if they were nothing more than Beaux-Arts exer-

[2] See Willard Connely, "New Chapters in the Life of Louis Sullivan," *Journal of the American Institute of Architects*, xx (September 1953), 111-13; Connely, *Louis Sullivan as He Lived* (New York, 1960), pp. 83-85; and the *Chicago Times*, May 21, 1876, p. 2.

[3] *Chicago Times*, May 21, 1876, p. 2.

[4] Sullivan, *Autobiography of an Idea*, pp. 197-202.

[5] *Genius*, p. 101.

[6] Connely, *Louis Sullivan as He Lived*, p. 60.

cises. Furthermore, the close resemblance of the Paris drawings to the drawings (Nos. 7-8) dated July 11, 1875, and therefore made after Sullivan's return to Chicago,[7] make it virtually certain that the Paris drawings have no relationship to Sullivan's work at the Beaux-Arts.

Sullivan's technique for making these drawings can be deduced from two pencil sketches for the Paris drawings that survive among the Lorch Papers. The original design for drawing No. 4 was made in pencil on a piece of heavy-weight drawing paper cut into an octagonal shape (Fig. 8). It shows the stylized bird and one of the two conventionalized plants. A tracing of the plant, now loose but originally glued to the octagonal paper, had been used by Sullivan to produce a symmetrical composition which then became the basic unit of a horizontal frieze. Sullivan's next step was to trace and ink the complete design to yield drawing No. 4. A drawing on the back of Sullivan's pencil study for No. 4 (Fig. 9) shows how he went about producing the designs he termed "center-pieces." By joining four tracings of the stalk near the base of each plant and inverting the leaves, he created a four-spoked roundel out of the same basic design. From this he must have made a tracing similar to No. 4 that has not survived.

To judge from the inscriptions, Sullivan considered his ink tracings the final product as far as he was concerned. Perhaps Edelmann had them enlarged by a draftsman into full-scale drawings or possibly the tracings passed to a decorating firm, which made full-size cartoons from them.

FIGURE DRAWINGS

9. A NUDE FIGURE, dated April 1, 1880.   FLLW/LHS No. 36

Inscribed in pencil: *4.1.80*. Annotations in pencil by Frank Lloyd Wright at the bottom: *#4 cut, (Vignette), FLLW*, and associated crop marks. Pencil on medium-weight drawing paper.
4 15/16 x 3 7/8 in.   12.6 x 9.9 cm.
Genius, with caption: *Early studies at the Beaux Arts dated 1880. Male figure after Michael Angelo.*

10. A NUDE FIGURE, dated May 30, 1880.   FLLW/LHS No. 38

Inscribed in pencil: *5.30.80*. Annotations in pencil by Frank Lloyd Wright on the right side: *cut*, and associated crop marks.
Pencil.
13 1/2 x 8 3/8 in.   34.2 x 21.2 cm.
Genius, with caption: *Early studies at the Beaux Arts dated 1880. Female figures from model.*

11. A NUDE FIGURE, dated Nov. 17, 1880.   FLLW/LHS No. 37

Inscribed in pencil: *11.17.80*. Annotations in pencil by Frank Lloyd Wright on the left side: *Full Page, cut*, and associated crop marks.

[7] Sullivan returned to Chicago from France in June 1875, according to A. T. Andreas, *History of* *Chicago* (3 vols.; Chicago, 1884), II, p. 566.

Pencil on tracing paper.
13 1/2 x 8 5/16 in.   34.2 x 21.1 cm.
Genius, with caption: *Early studies at the Beaux Arts dated 1880. Female figures from model.*

These studies belong to a group of twenty-two drawings of nude figures that Sullivan made between December 26, 1877, and August 30, 1885. In addition to the three at Avery, there are eighteen more in the collection of the Burnham Library and one in the Lorch Papers.[8]

It is unlikely that Sullivan made these drawings from live models in every case. The Michelangelesque or at least sixteenth-century character of a number of them, notably No. 11, would not ordinarily have resulted in working from a live model. That No. 11 is on tracing paper gives support to this idea. Even the drawing that seems most obviously made from a live model, because the figure's head is shown supported by a sling (Fig. 15), was executed on the least likely day of the year for a modeling studio to have been open in Chicago: Christmas Day, 1879.

Considering Sullivan's professed desire to break away from traditional architectural forms, it is surprising to see him devoting time to academic studies of this kind. It would be easy enough to attribute Sullivan's interest in such drawings to his training in Paris except that none goes back that far. Thus they coincide almost exactly with the period of John Edelmann's temporary return to Chicago,[9] and it may be that he was in some way responsible for Sullivan's interest in the nude figure.

WINEMAN HOUSE, CHICAGO, ILLINOIS

12. COLUMN CAPITAL, about July 1882.   FLLW/LHS No. 34

Legend in pencil: *Capital for Porch Columns. Residence for M. Winemann, Esq. D. Adler & Co., Archts.* Architectural notations in pencil: *5, Plan of cols.* Annotations in pencil by Frank Lloyd Wright: *#10, see note in dummy, top, cut,* and associated crop marks.
Pencil on heavy-weight drawing paper.
24 7/8 x 28 1/16 in.   63.1 x 70.9 cm.
Genius, with caption: *Early Adler Buildings. Terra cotta. Drafting for D. Adler and Company. Chicago. 1880.*

This is Sullivan's earliest surviving drawing for a three-dimensional architectural ornament that can be identified with an executed building. While it is true that two drawings for a similar kind of ornament predate this one—the first in the Burnham Library dated March 23, 1881 (Fig. 14), and the second, among the Lorch Papers dated April 16, 1881 (Fig. 13)—neither can be associated with a specific commission. Although

---

[8] Except for Sullivan's first drawing of a nude figure, dated December 26, 1877, and his last, dated Aug. 30, 1885, all his drawings of this subject are dated between Jan. 20, 1879, and Mar. 23, 1881.

[9] The date of Edelmann's return to Chicago in the late summer or fall of 1879 and of his departure for Cleveland early in 1881 are surmised from city directories, various references in Sullivan's autobiography, a dated drawing of Edelmann by Sullivan in the Burnham Library, and several miscellaneous references.

not dated, this drawing for the capital of a porch column was probably made between July 1. 1882, when Marx Wineman was issued a building permit for a house at 2544 Michigan Avenue in Chicago,[10] and May 1883, when he was living in the house.[11]

The drawing is unique in that it is the only surviving drawing to bear the legend "D. Adler & Co." Contrary to Sullivan's statement in his autobiography,[12] the firm of D. Adler & Company, in which Sullivan was made a one-third partner, was founded on May 1, not in 1880 but in 1882.[13] This drawing is thus especially important as evidence that D. Adler & Company was in business between May 1, 1882, and May 1, 1883, the latter being the day when the famous firm of Adler & Sullivan was established.[14]

The drawing is also of interest because it appears to be a full-size working drawing executed by Sullivan himself. As the Wineman House has been demolished, we cannot be absolutely certain about the scale but the size of the capital in the drawing (c. 1' x 3'), certainly seems to suggest its probable size. Sullivan's only other full-size working drawing in the Avery Library collection was made in 1895 for the angle blocks in the stair railings of the Chicago Stock Exchange Building (No. 61).

The drawing also provides the only example in the Avery Library collection of what we have called Sullivan's second ornamental style of 1879 to 1883.

McVICKER'S THEATER REMODELING, CHICAGO, ILLINOIS

13. INTERIOR WALL WITH BOXES,   FLLW/LHS No. 49
dated January 9, 1883.

Annotations in pencil by Frank Lloyd Wright: *cut*, and associated crop marks.
Pencil on drawing paper.
13 1/2 x 8 3/8 in.   34.2 x 21.2 cm.
Genius, with caption: *Boxes for first McVickers Theatre. Painted wood and gilded plaster. Adler and Sullivan. 1884-85.*

The date, January 9, 1883, recorded on the mount of this drawing agrees reasonably well with construction notices reporting that plans for remodeling McVicker's Theater were made in the spring of 1883.[15] The date may have been copied from an identifying legend discarded when the edges of the drawing were trimmed. If such a legend was originally part of the drawing, it would explain how Wright, who did not join Adler & Sullivan until 1888, was able to associate the drawing with the McVicker's commission of 1883.

The forms and details of the boxes illustrated in the drawing belong to the stylistic type developed during the 1870's from the Queen Anne, Victorian Gothic, Second Empire, and Eastlake styles. The result, a crude but progressive vernacular, provided Sulli-

---

[10] *American Architect*, XII (July 1, 1882), 11.
[11] *Chicago City Directory*, 1883.
[12] Sullivan, *Autobiography of an Idea*, pp. 256-57.
[13] City directory entries change from Dankmar Adler, Architect, to D. Adler & Co. (when Adler and Sullivan began their 2/3–1/3 partnership) with the directory of 1882, information for which was gathered during May and June 1882. Other evidence corroborates the directory entries.

[14] The firm of Adler & Sullivan is first listed in the city directory of 1883.
[15] *Inland Architect*, IV (September 1884), 28; V (January 1885); V (May 1885), 68.

van with the kind of inspiration he needed during the 1880's to move gradually forward toward an original style.

14. ORNAMENTAL DESIGN, dated May 6, 1884. FLLW/LHS No. 15

Inscribed in pencil: *5. 6. 84.* Annotations in pencil by Frank Lloyd Wright: crop marks.
Pencil.
13 11/16 x 8 3/8 in.   34.7 x 21.2 cm.
Genius, with caption: *Ornament detail. Gilded plaster. First McVickers Theatre. 1884-85.*

This is the only surviving drawing in what we have called Sullivan's third ornamental style, 1883-1885. Characteristic of the period is a complex integration of motifs. Now they are intertwined and overlapped instead of being carefully separated as in Sullivan's earlier work. Individual motifs also become more sinuous and flowing than before. This is especially evident in the graceful curves and undulating shapes of its stylized stems, leaves, flowers, and pods.

In *Genius* Wright calls this design for a gilded plaster detail in the first McVicker's Theater. Although there seems to be no existing evidence for his attribution, the date on the drawing conforms fairly well to what is known about the dates of McVicker's remodeling by Adler & Sullivan.[16] Perhaps this drawing, which apparently was trimmed to match No. 13, lost a legend associating it with McVicker's while still in Wright's possession.

ORNAMENTAL STUDIES

15. ORNAMENTAL STUDY, dated April 13, 1885. FLLW/LHS No. 21

Inscribed in pencil: *Alphabet. 4. 13. 85.* Annotations in pencil by Frank Lloyd Wright, at the bottom: *The beginning of the plastic period–85-G, #16,* and associated crop marks.
Pencil on paper torn from a pad.
10 7/8 x 6 15/16 in.   27.5 x 17.6 cm.
Genius, with caption: *Studies in plasticity. Terminology. Terra cotta. 1885.*

16. ORNAMENTAL STUDY, dated April 18, 1885. FLLW/LHS No. 13

Inscribed in pencil: *4. 18. 85.*
Pencil.
6 11/16 x 6 7/16 in.   17.0 x 16.4 cm.
Genius, with caption: *Studies in plasticity. Terminology. Terra cotta. 1885.*

17A. ORNAMENTAL STUDY, dated April 18, 1885. FLLW/LHS No. 14

Inscribed in pencil: *4. 18. 85.*
Pencil.
6 7/8 x 6 3/4 in.   17.4 x 17.1 cm.

[16] *Ibid.*

Genius, with caption: *Study. Beginning of the plastic period. 1885-86.* Obverse of No. 17B.

17B. ORNAMENTAL STUDY, dated April 18, 1885.   FLLW/LHS No. 14

Inscribed in pencil: *4. 18. 85.*
Pencil.
6 7/8 x 6 3/4 in.   17.4 x 17.1 cm.
Reverse of No. 17A.

18. ORNAMENTAL STUDY, dated April 18, 1885.   FLLW/LHS No. 125

Inscribed in pencil: *4. 18. 85.* Annotation in pencil by Frank Lloyd Wright in the upper left: *Chapter end.*
Pencil on paper torn from a pad.
3 x 7 in.   7.6 x 17.7 cm.

19. ORNAMENTAL STUDY, dated May 17, 1885.   FLLW/LHS No. 40

Inscribed in pencil: *Combined L and S. L motive. 5. 17. 85.* Annotations in pencil by Frank Lloyd Wright, at the bottom left: *#19, cut,* and associated crop marks.
Pencil on paper torn from a pad.
10 5/8 x 6 15/16 in.   27 x 17.7 cm.
Genius, with caption: *Study in Differentiation. Terra Cotta. 1885.*

20. ORNAMENTAL STUDY, dated August 23, 1885.   FLLW/LHS No. 4

Inscribed in pencil: *8. 23. 85.* Annotations in pencil by Frank Lloyd Wright, in the upper left corner: *please paint out this old crop line,* in the lower left: *#17, cut,* and associated crop marks.
Pencil on paper torn from a pad.
10 9/16 x 7 in.   26.8 x 17.7 cm.
Genius, with caption: *Studies in plasticity. Terra cotta. 1885.*

21. ORNAMENTAL STUDY, dated August 23, 1885.   FLLW/LHS No. 89

Inscribed in pencil: *Tribute 8. 23. 85.* Annotation in pencil by Frank Lloyd Wright on the right side: *Chapter end.*
Pencil.
6 15/16 x 10 1/2 in.   17.7 x 26.7 cm.
The two outer motifs are rubbings from the one in the center as the folds in the paper and the reversed images demonstrate.

22. ORNAMENTAL STUDY, dated August 28, 1885.   FLLW/LHS No. 5

Inscribed in pencil: *8. 28. 85.* Annotations in pencil by Frank Lloyd Wright, at the bottom: *#18, cut,* and associated crop marks.
Pencil.
5 3/8 x 3 7/8 in.   13.6 x 9.9 cm.
Genius, with caption: *Studies in plasticity. Terra cotta. 1885.*

23. ORNAMENTAL STUDY, dated December 18, 1885.   FLLW/LHS No. 22

Inscribed in pencil: *12. 18. 85. Motif.* Annotations in pencil by Frank Lloyd Wright: crop marks.
Pencil on paper torn from a pad.
10 3/4 x 6 15/16 in.   27.3 x 17.6 cm.
Reverse of No. 25A.
Genius, with caption: *Plasticity. Study for terra cotta. 1885.*

These drawings form a connected series of what appear to be experimental studies unrelated to architectural commissions. Five of them come from a pad of paper (7 x 11 inches) perforated along its inner edge for ease in removing the sheets. The others may have come from the same pad but as they have been trimmed it is not possible to be certain. An ornamental drawing of Oct. 19, 1885, given by Sullivan to Earl H. Reed in 1913 but now in the Burnham Library, apparently also belongs to the same series. Although Sullivan may have made similar informal study sketches throughout his career, the large number surviving from 1885 (and the absence of similar sketches from other years) suggests that this series of drawings is without parallel in Sullivan's work.

It is evident that these sketches represent a shift in direction and emphasis. That Wright sensed in them a distinct caesura in the evolution of Sullivan's ornament, is clear from his notation on the earliest of them (No. 15): "The beginning of the plastic period." These drawings, in which a moving sinuous line creates the form, are especially carefree and unrestrained when compared with Sullivan's earlier drawings. Their plant motifs are also much closer to nature than previously. Possibly they reflect Sullivan's growing and—perhaps by 1885—urgent desire to perfect as quickly as possible an ornamental style uniquely his own.

On several of the drawings the meanings of Sullivan's inscriptions—"Alphabet," "Tribute," and "Combined L and S. L Motive"—are not known. Perhaps they relate to formulas with which he was experimenting for designing ornament.

Wright's notation "Chapter end" on Nos. 18 and 21 presumably relates to a projected mock-up of *Genius* that was not used. There are other indications of this: his note on No. 20, "please paint out this old crop line," and his numbers on many of the drawings which do not match the sequence in *Genius*.

There is no evidence in the drawings themselves to support Wright's contention, expressed as fact in the captions of *Genius*, that many of the drawings in this group were prepared for casting in terra cotta.

ORNAMENTAL DESIGN

24. ORNAMENTAL DESIGN, dated September 30, 1885.   FLLW/LHS No. 20

Inscribed in pencil: *9. 30. 85.*
Pencil.
10 1/2 x 6 9/16 in.   26.6 x 16.7 cm.
Genius, with caption: *Plaster panel for first McVickers Theatre. 1885.*

In contrast to the other drawings of 1885, this one seems, in its symmetry, precise shading, and disciplined linear rhythms, to have been prepared for execution. The sources of its complexly interwoven organic motifs are Sullivan's studies of earlier the same year (Nos. 15-22).

Frank Lloyd Wright believed this drawing was made for the remodeling of Mc-Vicker's Theater, an unlikely possibility, however, as McVicker's re-opened July 1, 1885,[17] nearly three months before the drawing was made.

COVER FOR THE CATALOGUE OF A WHOLESALE DRUGGIST

25A. COVER DESIGN, about 1887.   FLLW/LHS No. 22

As part of the design there is the legend in pencil: *Robert S . . . . Co.*; and in the buds at the top: *Co* and *R . . . S . . .*
Pencil on paper torn from a pad.
10 3/4 x 6 15/16 in.   27.3 x 17.6 cm.
Reverse of No. 23.

25B. COVER DESIGN, dated January 25, 1887.   FLLW/LHS No. 92

Inscribed in pencil: *1. 25. 87.* As part of the design there is the legend lettered in pencil: *Robert Stevenson & Co. Vol. II. Wholesale Druggists.*
Pencil.
10 11/16 x 7 in.   27.1 x 17.7 cm.

Although Sullivan seems to have thought of his decorative art as a system specifically developed for architectural surfaces, he would sometimes provide a design, of which this is the earliest surviving example, for a purpose quite unrelated to architecture. In doing so, he was, of course, acting according to precedents established by William Morris and the English Arts and Crafts movement. The earliest recorded design of this kind by Sullivan was made about 1881 for a wallpaper but neither his design nor the wallpaper survives.[18] Sullivan differed from his English contemporaries in that they were concerned with improving design—architectural or otherwise—for its own sake, whereas Sullivan was committed to improving design almost exclusively in its architectural applications. Such designs as this title page represent no more than a marginal part of Sullivan's work, evidently made only when specifically requested by a friend or client.

By comparing Sullivan's sketchy preliminary study (No. 25A) for the druggist's catalogue with his carefully worked out final design, we can observe Sullivan's method of shifting and integrating motifs until a balanced and well-proportioned effect was achieved. In making both drawings, Sullivan apparently used the same pad of paper (7 x 11 inches) that served him for his studies of 1885 (Nos. 15-23). In fact, his preliminary sketch for the cover is on the back of drawing No. 23.

According to the *Chicago Business Directory* for 1889 the Stevenson firm of wholesale druggists was located at 92 Lake Street. It is not known if the design was actually used for their catalogue.

[17] John Flynn, *The Standard Guide to Chicago* (Chicago, 1892), p. 127.   [18] *American Architect*, XXIII (February 11, 1888), 71.

AUDITORIUM BUILDING, CHICAGO, ILLINOIS

Plaster Corbels

26. ORNAMENTAL CORBEL,   (Fig. 16)   FLLW/LHS No. 51
dated July 23, 1888.

Legend in pencil: *Elevations of Corbel under Plaster Beams. Adler & Sullivan. July 23/88. Chicago Auditorium Building. Scale 1 1/2 inch = One Foot.* Dimensions in pencil.
Pencil on heavy-weight drawing paper.
10 x 9 7/8 in.   25.3 x 25.1 cm.

This corbel with its long, gracefully curving leaves, linear tendrils curling into spirals, and unopened flowers is typical of Sullivan's ornament in the Auditorium Building. As the only dated drawing surviving for an ornamental detail in that building, it helps to corroborate other evidence pointing to 1888 as the year when most of the interior decorations were worked out.
The drawing is also of interest because it is the earliest example of a working drawing made to scale by Sullivan.[19] The scale used for the drawing of one and one-half inches to the foot was preferred by Sullivan for working drawings of ornament.

27. ORNAMENTAL CORBEL, 1888-1889.   FLLW/LHS No. 9

Pencil.
7 7/8 x 4 in.   20.0 by 10.1 cm.
Genius, with caption: *Corbel for the Auditorium. Plaster. 1887-88.*

This drawing is unusual in being a perspective study instead of the more typical elevation. In *Genius*, Wright identified it as the design for a corbel in the Auditorium Building, but no ornament in the building corresponds exactly to it.

Mosaics

28. MOSAIC STAIR LANDING, 1888-1889.   (Fig. 17)   FLLW/LHS No. 64

Inscribed in pencil: *Hotel Landing.*
Pencil on paper torn from a pad.
3 1/4 x 7 3/4 in.   8.3 x 19.7 cm.

29. MOSAIC STAIR LANDING, 1888-1889.   (Fig. 18)   FLLW/LHS No. 121

Inscribed in pencil: *Upper.* Notation in design on right: *Same.*
Pencil on paper torn from a pad.
5 1/2 x 6 15/16 in.   13.9 x 17.6 cm.

[19] Sullivan's earlier working drawing of about 1882 for the porch capitals of the Wineman House (No. 12) is not in the same class because it is drawn full size instead of to a scale. The same is true of his tracings for stencils of the mid 1870's (Nos. 4-8), which are really working drawings even though they are not scaled.

30A. MOSAIC WALL DECORATION,   (Fig. 19)   FLLW/LHS No. 91
1888-1889.

Inscribed in pencil: *Inglenook*.
Pencil.
5 1/2 x 7 3/4 in.   13.9 x 19.6 cm.
Obverse of 30B.

30B. MOSAIC DECORATION [?], 1888-1889.   FLLW/LHS No. 91

Pencil.
5 1/2 x 7 3/4 in.   13.9 x 19.6 cm.
Reverse of 30A.

Nos. 28 and 29 are designs for the first- and second-floor stair landings in the Auditorium Hotel. No. 30A is a study for the wall mosaic in the north inglenook of the Auditorium Theater lobby. No. 30B may be an unused study for a mosaic also intended for the Theater lobby.

Sullivan's only earlier preserved drawings for two-dimensional ornaments are the ones he made for frescoes in the mid 1870's (Nos. 2-8). The differences between the two groups are quite marked however, for where Sullivan's fresco designs were models of a restrained linear technique, these later studies for mosaics are, by comparison, improvised graphic cadenzas. Although these differences are partly stylistic, they can be largely attributed to the stage of design that each group represents. Thus those for frescoes, even though not scaled, are essentially working drawings while the ones for mosaics are surely initial studies. By the time these sketches for mosaics were re-drawn by Sullivan and then converted into working drawings by his staff, they must have lost most of their lyrical and poetic qualities and became, like the mosaics executed from them (Figs. 17-19), simplified in shape, and precise in outline.

As executed these mosaics are entirely two-dimensional with no hint of illusionary space. In them Sullivan sought to modify his floral abstractions so that they retained the style and flavor of his three-dimensional work without violating the two-dimensional integrity of the flat surface. Indeed, it is only by the stylistic continuity between Sullivan's plastic and flat decorations that we can feel confident that two-dimensional designs, like these mosaics, are by Sullivan himself and not the work of interior decorators. There are, for example, other mosaics as well as stained-glass and stencils in the Auditorium Building which, while sympathetic to Sullivan's three-dimensional style, do not seem to be two-dimensional modifications of it. Concerning these, we know that a firm of decorators was employed to design as well as execute many of the stencils, mosaics, and stained-glass windows in the Auditorium Building.[20] Thus in the Auditorium, as in other buildings by Adler & Sullivan, whenever there is not an intimate stylistic continuity between the flat and plastic ornaments, we should be suspicious that the flat decorations, while probably approved by Sullivan, were not designed by him.

[20] The principals of Healy & Millet were personal friends of Sullivan; see *Inland Architect*, IX (July 1888), 89.

34

BRONZE NEWEL POST

31. NEWEL POST, 1888.   (Fig. 21)   FLLW/LHS No. 94

Pencil on tracing paper.
9 3/4 x 8 3/16 in.   24.7 x 20.8 cm.
Not drawn by Sullivan.

This fragment of a tracing matches one published by Wright in *Drawings for a Living Architecture*.[21] On it Wright wrote, "Fragment of Bronze Newel post, hotel, Auditorium, Chicago." The design was used for newel posts in the Hotel and Theater and was, according to Wright, one of his very first assignments after joining Adler & Sullivan.[22]

Wright was hired in 1888 to assist in detailing or working up Sullivan's sketches for the ornaments of the Auditorium Building. Before that commission Adler & Sullivan's business was much more modest and Sullivan probably did much of his own detailing as, for example, the porch capitals of the Wineman House (No. 12). Wright's job from 1888 on seems to have been to enlarge Sullivan's sketches into scale working drawings, sometimes to full size as here, to trace the working drawings onto linen, and to make the necessary prints from them. In the case of the newel post, Sullivan must not have found Wright's tracing entirely to his satisfaction for it differs in several respects from the existing newel posts (Fig. 21) and we may conclude that Sullivan rejected it.

BANQUET HALL, AUDITORIUM BUILDING, CHICAGO, ILLINOIS

32. ORNAMENTAL CAPITAL,   (Fig. 22)   FLLW/LHS No. 88
dated April 15, 1890.

Legend in pencil at the lower left: *Banquet Hall Cap. A & S. 4/15/90.* In the lower right corner there is figuring: *3)48(16* and *2)36(18.*
Pencil.
5 3/8 x 8 1/4 in.   13.7 x 20.6 cm.

33. ORNAMENTAL CAPITAL,   (Fig. 23)   FLLW/LHS No. 50
dated July 10, 1890.

Legend in pencil at bottom: *Banquet Hall (corner) Cap. No. 15. Adler & Sullivan. July 10/90.* Notations in pencil on the left: *Neck 7", Soffit 11", Face 13",* on the right: *These divisions are 2" each, Mitre of Soffit, Curve between soffit and neck, Rounded Corner,* and dimensions. Annotations in pencil by Frank Lloyd Wright, at the bottom: *Cut in paper edge, FLLW,* and associated crop marks.
Pencil.
7 1/8 x 7 5/16 in.   18.1 x 18.5 cm. (size of top sheet only)

[21] (New York, 1959), p. 154.
[22] Crombie Taylor, architect in charge of restoring the Auditorium Banquet Hall, relates that Wright told him the newel post was his first assignment after joining Adler & Sullivan.

Genius, with caption: *One of a series of fifteen carved wood capitals. Glued-up mahogany blocks. Auditorium banquet hall. 1890.*

34. ORNAMENTAL CAPITAL,   (Fig. 24)   FLLW/LHS No. 53
dated July 17, 1890.

Legend in pencil at bottom: *Banquet Hall Cap No 16. Adler & Sullivan. July 17/90. Scale 1 1/2" = 1 foot.* Sullivan's monogram. Notations in pencil, on the left side: *Neck 7", Soffit 11", Facia 13",* at the top: *Return 3.1" to Cut against wall, Face 4.0",* on the right side: *Mitre line, Curve, Round corner,* on the soffit, left and right: *Same,* and dimensions.
Pencil.
8 1/2 x 7 5/8 in.   21.6 x 19.4 cm.
Sullivan's monogram appears for the first time on this drawing.

During the spring and summer of 1890 Adler & Sullivan added to the completed Auditorium Building a banquet hall suspended on metal trusses over the orchestra of the auditorium. These drawings for carved-wood capitals in the hall demonstrate that Sullivan thought of his ornament as a universal system for carving as well as modeling. In fact, Sullivan's drawing of a terracotta panel for the Kehilath Anshe Ma'ariv Synagogue (No. 35), executed by modeling and molding, is virtually identical in date, style, and technique with Sullivan's drawings of the Banquet Hall capitals despite the very different materials and manner of execution. Wright would later object to Sullivan's propensity to treat all materials alike without regard for what Wright believed the innate qualities of each material.[23] But to recall Wright's criticism is not to imply that either Wright or his predecessors had discovered the truth about ornamental and architectural design in an absolute sense: obviously architects in many past epochs bent materials to their will and, certainly in Sullivan's case, we are much the richer for it.

With the Banquet Hall capitals we reach the next phase of Sullivan's decorative development and the beginning of his ornamental maturity. The most striking difference between these ornaments of 1890 and those of the 1880's is the introduction in the capitals of geometrical motifs. Instead of a purely organic ornament, we now have an ornament in which organic and geometrical motifs are mingled. The spiky-edged leaf of the Auditorium years, while still in evidence, is shortly to be superseded by an acanthus-shaped leaf (Fig. 22). Its disappearance during 1890 marks the end of those hard, angular, conventionalized motifs that so largely characterized Sullivan's decorative work from 1874 through 1889. Certainly by the end of 1890, but beginning with the Banquet Hall capitals, Sullivan achieved a genuinely masterful integration of organic and geometrical forms in compositions so sophisticated as to signify that his ornament had at last reached maturity. No longer is there the slightest hesitation or uncertainty; from here on, Sullivan's designs are on the highest plane of skillful modulation and refinement.

The ornamental capitals made from these drawings were carved in red birch, not mahogany as Wright claims. They still occupy their original positions in what was the banquet hall of the Auditorium Building, now Ganz Hall of Roosevelt University. These

[23] *Genius*, p. 74.

capitals should be high on the list of priorities for those who derive visual pleasure from Sullivan's ornament.

KEHILATH ANSHE MA'ARIV SYNAGOGUE, CHICAGO, ILLINOIS

35. ORNAMENTAL PANEL,   (Fig. 25)   FLLW/LHS No. 52
    dated June 19, 1890.

> Legend in pencil: *T. C. Panel for Synagogue. Adler & Sullivan. 6/19/90.* Notations in pencil, at the bottom: *Panel 4.6″ long, 4.0″ high*; and in the design: *over, under, 1/2″ break.*
> Pencil.
> 10 1/4 x 8 1/4 in.   26.0 x 21.0 cm.

The terra-cotta panels for which this drawing was made are still *in situ* on the west front of the building (Fig. 25), now the Pilgrim Baptist Church, located at the southeast corner of Indiana Avenue and Thirty-third Street in Chicago. As originally conceived, these panels would have provided welcome textural accents in a facade designed as a geometric simplification in ashlar of Richardson's rock-face Romanesque style.[24] But in the building as executed, with its small-scale rock-face surfaces, the original purpose of these panels is lost and they are of interest today only as isolated ornamental designs.

ORNAMENTAL DESIGNS

36. ORNAMENTAL DESIGN, about 1890.   FLLW/LHS No. 83

> Inscribed in pencil: *Carved Wainscot, Drawing for* . . . [illegible], *FLLW.* Dimensions in pencil.
> Pencil on tracing paper.
> 9 3/8 x 4 in.   23.8 x 10.2 cm.
> Not drawn by Sullivan.

This drawing on tracing paper is signed by Frank Lloyd Wright and bears an inscription in his handwriting which appears to read, "Carved Wainscot, Drawing for . . ." with the last and probably crucial word illegible. Although surely traced from a drawing by Sullivan, the result lacks the clarity of form and preciseness of line characteristic of Sullivan's own work.

That the wainscot may date from the year 1890 is suggested by its close resemblance, if rotated clockwise ninety degrees, to a capital of that year in the Auditorium Banquet Hall (No. 32; Fig. 22). Although there is a carved wainscot in the Banquet Hall, none of its purely geometric sawed-wood patterns is related to this more ornate floral design. In any event, the illegible word cannot very easily be made to refer to this commission.

[24] For illustrations see Hugh Morrison, *Louis Sullivan*, figs. 34-35.

37. DESIGN FOR AN ORNAMENTAL FRAME, FLLW/LHS No. 31
about 1890.

Pencil on tracing paper.
20 7/8 x 19 3/4 in.   52.8 x 50.0 cm.

Even though not dated, this tracing is clearly in Sullivan's ornamental style of 1890-1891. Its details resemble most closely the bronze door of the Getty Tomb designed late in 1890. This resemblance and, more importantly, the intermingling of geometric and botanical forms rule out its being a study for one of the paintings in the Auditorium, which at first glance it seems to resemble very closely. It also exceeds in sophistication and complexity all of the Auditorium ornaments, for which reason alone it would seem to date from a later, more mature period. The drawing could have been intended for the Auditorium of the Seattle Opera House, designed at the same time as the Getty Tomb but not built except for the foundations.

No doubt Sullivan used tracing paper in this instance as a compositional device for bringing together ornamental and figural drawings originally sketched on separate sheets of paper. The tracing probably survives because, in not being used, Sullivan retained it instead of passing it on to his chief draftsman for working up at larger scale.

GETTY TOMB, CHICAGO, ILLINOIS

38. ORNAMENTAL CORNICE,   (Fig. 26) FLLW/LHS No. 25
dated October 16, 1890.

Legend in pencil: *Getty Tomb. Oct 16/90.* Notation in pencil in the upper left: *Carving.* There is figuring in pencil in the lower left corner. Annotations in pencil by Frank Lloyd Wright, on the left: *bleed,* at the top, left side, and bottom: *cut,* and associated crop marks.
Pencil on the back of a sheet of Adler & Sullivan stationery (left side) attached to a piece of plain paper (right side).
8 5/16 x 17 5/16 in.   21.1 x 43.9 cm.
Genius, with caption: *Carving of lower edge of granite arch, face and soffit. Getty Tomb. Graceland Cemetery, Chicago. 1890-91.*

39. ORNAMENTAL ARCH,   (Fig. 27) FLLW/LHS No. 29
about October 1890.

Notations in pencil, in the center: *joint,* on the right: *soffit, Radius 2", 4" return,* and towards the bottom center: *inside to outside.* Annotations in pencil by Frank Lloyd Wright, in the lower right: *double pg. spread, see note in dummy,* at bottom: *#27,* at top and bottom: *cut,* and associated crop marks.
Pencil on heavy-weight drawing paper.
20 5/16 x 24 in.   51.3 x 60.8 cm.
Not drawn by Sullivan.
Genius, with caption: *Full size detail of stone carving of face and soffit of arch. Getty Tomb. 1890-91.*

Of the two surviving drawings for the Getty Tomb, only the one of its cornice is in Sullivan's hand. Sullivan's sketch for the cornice (No. 38) consists of interwoven geometric and botanical motifs of the type characteristic of Sullivan's mature ornament during 1890-1891. The varied lights and darks produced by Sullivan's pencil remain so fresh and spontaneous that the pattern seems almost to continue its evolution before our eyes. In the drawing there is an immediacy, typical of so many ornamental sketches by Sullivan, that suggests its lines were laid down in an inspired moment. Indeed, the paper on which Sullivan worked, made up of a sheet of imprinted office stationery attached to a piece of plain paper, implies a certain urgency on his part as if trying to capture a vision that was quickly evaporating.

The other drawing showing the details of the entrance arch (No. 39) is at full scale. Its author may be Wright, who in his role as chief draftsman would normally have enlarged Sullivan's sketches to the required scale. From this drawing Wright would have made a linen tracing and from that tracing the required blueprints. That in this drawing all of the facileness and verve of Sullivan's pencil-sketches should be lacking is easy to understand. Even if Wright had had Sullivan's enthusiasm for sketching, the need of the stone carver for solid well-shaded details would have denied Wright the luxury of so spontaneous a drawing.

The carved limestone ornaments for which these drawings were made can still be seen on the Getty Tomb in Graceland Cemetery, Chicago.

McVICKER'S THEATER REMODELING, CHICAGO, ILLINOIS

40. ORNAMENTAL SOFFIT, dated December 9, 1890.   FLLW/LHS No. 46

Legend in pencil: *McVickers Theatre. Adler & Sullivan. Plaster Ornament. Soffit of Proscenium Arch. Band No. 1. Dec. 9/90.* Notations in pencil, toward bottom: *Center line*, and dimensions. Annotations in pencil by Frank Lloyd Wright, at the top and upper left side: *text line*, and associated crop marks.
Pencil.
11 13/16 x 8 1/4 in.   30.0 x 21.0 cm.
Genius, with caption: *Similar design for second McVickers Theatre dated 1890* [Wright is contrasting the drawing with another (No. 96) for a column in the Guaranty Building]. *Technique contrasting with later rendering of parallel drawing dated 1895.*

41. ORNAMENTAL BALCONY FRONT   FLLW/LHS No. 39
dated December 25, 1890.

Legend in pencil: *McVicker's Theatre. Adler & Sullivan, Archts. Plaster Ornamentation of Balcony Front. Scale 1/8" = 1' [sic]. Dec. 25/90.* Notations in pencil, right side, top and bottom: *wood moulding*, and dimensions. Annotations by Frank Lloyd Wright, top and left: *cut*, and associated crop marks.
Pencil.
7 1/2 x 11 1/2 in.   19.0 x 29.1 cm.
Genius, with caption: *Balcony front. Plaster. Electric light set in ornament. McVickers Theatre rebuilt. 1890.*

42. ORNAMENTAL PANEL, (Fig. 29)   FLLW/LHS No. 54
dated January 26, 1891.

Legend in pencil: *McVickers Theatre. Adler & Sullivan. Circular Panel in Proscenium. Jan. 26/91.* Notation in pencil in the design: *R = 2'6 1/4″*, and dimensions.
Pencil.
10 1/2 x 8 1/4 in.   26.5 x 21.0 cm.

43. ORNAMENTAL RIB, (Fig. 28)   FLLW/LHS No. 42
dated January 27, 1891.

Legend in pencil: *McVickers Theatre. Adler & Sullivan. Rib ornament No. 3. Jan. 27th, 91.* Dimensions in pencil. Annotations in pencil by Frank Lloyd Wright, at the top, left side and bottom: *cut,* and associated crop marks.
Pencil.
10 x 8 1/2 in.   25.4 x 21.5 cm.
Not drawn by Sullivan.
Genius, with caption: *One of the nine plaster bands on sounding board of proscenium. McVickers Theatre rebuilt. 1890-91.*

44. ORNAMENTAL BAND, (Fig. 28)   FLLW/LHS No. 45
dated February 2, 1891.

Legend in pencil: *McVickers Theatre. Adler & Sullivan. Band No [2]. Feb 2/91.* Dimensions in pencil. Annotation in pencil by Frank Lloyd Wright on the left side: *cut.*
Pencil.
10 x 8 3/8 in.   25.5 x 21.2 cm.
Genius, with caption: *One of the nine ornamental bands on sounding board of proscenium. Plaster. McVickers Theatre rebuilt. 1890-91.*

45. ORNAMENTAL BAND, 1890-1891. (Fig. 28)   FLLW/LHS No. 47

Legend in pencil: *McVickers Theatre. Adler & Sullivan, Archts. Plaster Ornament in Sounding board. Band No. 4.* Notations in pencil at top: *Center line,* and dimensions. Annotations in pencil by Frank Lloyd Wright, at the bottom: *bleed, #29,* on the left: *cut,* and associated crop marks.
Pencil.
12 1/4 x 5 3/8 in.   31.0 x 13.6 cm.
Genius, with caption: *One of the nine ornamental bands on sounding board of proscenium. Plaster. McVickers Theatre rebuilt. 1890-91.*

46. ORNAMENTAL BAND, 1890-1891.   FLLW/LHS No. 6

Legend in pencil: *[McVicker's] Theatre. Adler & Sullivan.* Annotations in pencil by Frank Lloyd Wright: crop marks.
Pencil.
7 3/8 x 5 1/2 in.   18.7 x 14.0 cm.
Ornamental band No. 8 in the sounding board.

Genius, with caption: [One of] *Two plaster soffits. Transportation Building, Chicago World's Fair. 1892/93. [sic]*.

47. ORNAMENTAL RIB, 1890-1891. (Fig. 28)   FLLW/LHS No. 3

Annotations in pencil by Frank Lloyd Wright, on the left side and at the bottom: *cut*, and associated crop marks.
Pencil on paper torn from a pad.
7 1/2 x 7 13/16 in.   19.1 x 19.8 cm.
Rib ornament No. 4 in the sounding board.
Not drawn by Sullivan.
Genius, with caption: *One of the nine plaster bands on sounding board of proscenium. McVickers Theatre rebuilt. 1890-91.*

48. ORNAMENTAL FRIEZE, 1890-1891.   FLLW/LHS No. 43

Legend in pencil: *McVickers Theatre. Frieze in Foyer*. Annotations in pencil by Frank Lloyd Wright on the left and bottom: *cut*, in legend: *18?*, and associated crop marks.
Pencil on paper torn from a pad.
12 x 8 1/2 in.   30.5 x 21.5 cm.
Not drawn by Sullivan.
Genius, with caption: *Frieze in foyer. Plaster. McVickers Theatre rebuilt. 1891.*

49. ORNAMENTAL RIB [?], 1890-1891.   FLLW/LHS No. 90

Pencil.
7 9/16 x 7 7/8 in.   19.2 x 19.9 cm.
McVicker's Theater [?].
Not drawn by Sullivan.

50. ORNAMENTAL RIB [?], 1890-1891.   FLLW/LHS No. 24

Pencil.
10 13/16 x 8 7/16 in.   27.4 x 21.5 cm.
McVicker's Theater [?].
Not drawn by Sullivan.

During the winter of 1890-1891 Adler & Sullivan worked almost uninterruptedly on drawings for remodeling the interior of McVicker's Theater after the disastrous fire of August 1890. The pressure under which Sullivan labored is suggested by the dates on these ornamental drawings, one of which (No. 41) was made on Christmas Day, 1890.

Although McVicker's Theater as remodeled by Adler & Sullivan no longer stands, the original positions of nearly all its ornaments for which drawings survive can be established from old photographs of the interior (Fig. 28). A majority of them were for the plaster decorations covering the surfaces of the sounding board. Adler & Sullivan used similar bands of ornament in nearly every auditorium they designed. The purpose of the ornament was not only decorative for it also served to break up and absorb undesirable sound waves. Compared with other acoustical shells designed by the firm, this one, in being rectilinear rather than elliptical, was very unusual. The rest of the drawings were for the ornamental surfaces of the proscenium arch, balcony front, and foyer.

Sullivan seems to have followed no logical sequence in making these sketches. Although he began on December 9 with Band No. 1 (No. 40), which was the soffit of the proscenium arch, he did not design the decoration in the spandrels of that arch until January 26 (No. 42), nor did he make a sketch for Band No. 2 until February 2 (No. 44). Perhaps this shifting around was related in some way to the vicissitudes of construction.

No doubt it was the crush of work during the winter of 1890-1891 that led Sullivan to re-use one of his designs for McVicker's Theater in the Kehilath Anshe Ma'ariv Synagogue. That the circular panels in the sanctuary arch of the synagogue (Fig. 29) are derived from the McVicker's remodeling and not the other way around, is clear from Sullivan's McVicker's sketch, which is obviously an initial study and is labeled "Circular Panel in Proscenium, McVicker's Theatre."

Two drawings (Nos. 49-50) without identifying inscriptions and which cannot be closely associated with any known ornaments by Sullivan, may have been made for McVicker's Theater. Although technically crude, and thus certainly not by Sullivan, they resemble in their proportions, in their vertical orientation, and in the way their patterns are developed the rib ornaments on the sounding board of McVicker's. Three other ornamental drawings (Nos. 43, 47-48), all of them for identifiable parts of the McVicker's ornamentation, seem technically inferior to Sullivan's authenticated drawings. All five drawings are thus most likely the work of Sullivan's assistants.

As these drawings are sketches, and not the working drawings ordinarily produced by Sullivan's staff, it would appear that during the busy winter of 1890-1891 Sullivan was forced to delegate to his staff a part of the design process normally reserved for himself. That the increased responsibility Sullivan allowed his subordinates was to work out his original sketches in greater detail and not to design the ornaments themselves, is suggested by the drawing for rib ornament No. 3 (No. 43). Although at first glance this drawing may seem to be an initial design, it was in fact developed from an original sketch by Sullivan that at one time was in the Wright collection but is now lost (Fig. 30).[25]

Another drawing also missing from the Wright collection when it passed to the Avery Library is Sullivan's study for Band No. 5 of the McVicker's sounding board. Wright illustrated it in *Genius* with the erroneous caption: "One of nine continuous plaster bands two feet wide on sounding board of proscenium." There were actually only six plaster bands of approximately that width on the sounding board (Fig. 28). They were separated by five ribs 10 inches wide—some of which Wright also calls bands—and framed by two narrow bands decorated with a geometric ornament. At the outer end of the sounding board there was also a continuous ornamental band (No. 46) 30 inches in width. According to the drawings Sullivan numbered these bands outward from the stage beginning with the soffit of the proscenium arch (No. 40) for a total of eight bands. His numbering of the ribs, which came to seven, also started at the proscenium arch. No matter how these bands and ribs are added together, they cannot very easily be made to equal the nine remembered by Wright.

[25] This drawing was photographed by Richard Nickel at Taliesin, Frank Lloyd Wright's home in Wisconsin, in the 1950's.

WAINWRIGHT BUILDING, ST. LOUIS, MISSOURI

51. ORNAMENTAL PANEL, (Fig. 32)   FLLW/LHS No. 122
dated April 17, [1891].

Legend in pencil: *T.*[erra] *C.*[otta] *Panels. Wainwright Bldg. A*[dler] *& S*[ullivan], *C*[harles] *L R*[amsey], *A.*[ssociated] *A*[rchitects]. *April 17/*[91]. Notation in pencil below design: *Under 7th Story Sill.* Annotations in pencil by Frank Lloyd Wright, at the left: *cut, #29,* and associated crop marks.
Pencil.
7 1/4 x 4 1/2 in.   18.5 x 11.5 cm.
Genius, with caption: *Terra cotta panel between windows. Wainwright Building, Buffalo* [*sic*]. *1891.*

The terra-cotta panel for which this drawing was made can still be seen, as the legend states, under the seventh story sill of the Wainwright Building at the Northwest corner of Seventh and Chestnut Streets, St. Louis (Fig. 32). The time interval between the design of a large building like the Wainwright and the detailing of its exterior ornament can be estimated by comparing the date of this drawing, April 17, 1891, with the date, November 19, 1890, when a notice published in the Chicago *Economist* reported that plans were being made.[26] It indicates that as many as five months might have separated the planning of a large building and the detailing of its exterior.

Charles Ramsey (1845-1913) was a St. Louis architect with whom Adler & Sullivan associated whenever they had a commission in that city.

TRANSPORTATION BUILDING, COLUMBIAN
EXPOSITION, CHICAGO

52. ORNAMENTAL DOOR JAMB, (Fig. 33)   FLLW/LHS No. 7
dated September 23, 1891.

Legend in pencil: *Transportation Bldg. Soffit of Main Arch. Sept. 23-91.* Dimensions in pencil. Annotations in pencil by Frank Lloyd Wright, on the left: *cut,* at the bottom: *#35, cut,* on the right: *6 7/8,* and associated crop marks.
Pencil.
6 13/16 x 4 3/16 in.   17.3 x 10.6 cm.
Genius, with caption: [One of] *Two plaster soffits. Transportation Building, Chicago World's Fair. 1892-93.*

53. ORNAMENTAL FOUNTAIN, 1891. (Fig. 34)   FLLW/LHS No. 27

Notations in pencil, upper left in design: *ornament returned on soffit, continued,* on the right spandrel: *same Reversed,* on the lower left of fountain: *Bas Relief here,* and below the lion head: *dentils.*
Pencil on heavy-weight drawing paper.
19 7/8 x 24 in.   50.3 x 60.8 cm.

[26] IV (Nov. 29, 1890), 900.

54. ORNAMENTAL FRESCO, 1892.

FLLW/LHS No. 28

Notation in pencil, at the upper right: *Bands Continued*.
Pencil on tracing paper.
18 x 17 5/8 in.   45.7 x 44.6 cm.
Tracing not by Sullivan.

The ornaments depicted in the drawings for the door jamb (No. 52) and the fountain (No. 53) belong stylistically to Sullivan's ornament of 1890-1891. The date on No. 52 (September 23, 1891) follows the first publication of plans for the building by some four months and indicates that the plaster ornamentation of the building was designed during the late summer and autumn of that year. The fresco drawing (No. 54), on the other hand, is related stylistically to Sullivan's more geometrical ornament of 1892-1894 and thus must not have been designed until 1892. That this should have been the design sequence seems entirely reasonable as the application of plastic ornamentation would normally precede the painted decorations.

The drawing for the door jamb (No. 52) is especially interesting because in it Sullivan has interwoven floral, geometric, and human motifs (Fig. 33). Although Sullivan generally avoided human and animal images in his ornamental work, they do appear from time to time. Occasionally they are stylized like the bird in his early fresco (No. 4), or the winged female figure in the drawing for the Transportation Building (No. 54), but more often, as in No. 52 (Fig. 33), they are presented with a high degree of realism. Sullivan seems to have conventionalized his botanical, animal, and human subjects in his decorations of a two-dimensional character—fresco, mosaic, and stained-glass—with the result that there is a consistent and relatively high degree of abstraction always present in his work of this type. But when it came to plastic ornament, he frequently used more naturalistic botanical types and, along with them, highly representational human and animal forms. Given the subsequent evolution of decorative art, Sullivan's flat ornament seems more progressive than his plastic work. In any case, his Transportation Building, and the drawings surviving for its decoration, provide exceptionally good examples of both types.

Sullivan's drawing for the fountains (No. 53) incorporated in the small pavilions that bore sculptural groups projecting at intervals from the main front of the Transportation Building also combines floral, animal, and human motifs (Fig. 34). The realistic lion head of each fountain served in the conventional manner for conveying water through its mouth to the basin below. The nude figures in the spandrels follow the academic types Sullivan had been fond of sketching in the late 1870's and early 1880's (Nos. 9-11). Sullivan re-used the design of the plaster lunette above the lion head for the decorative stone arch (Fig. 35) over the front door of the house that he and his brother Albert began about September 1891 for their mother.[27]

The drawing for the exterior frescoes (No. 54) is not in Sullivan's hand. As it is of a relatively large size and on tracing paper, it was probably made by an assistant, perhaps Wright, for the purpose of combining several of Sullivan's designs into a single drawing preparatory to working it out in detail at a larger scale.

[27] Although the house—4575 Lake Park Avenue, Chicago—has been demolished, its ornamental front including the lunette over the door is preserved by Southern Illinois University at Edwardsville, Illinois.

WAINWRIGHT TOMB, ST. LOUIS, MISSOURI

55. ORNAMENTAL DOOR FRAME, 1892.   FLLW/LHS No. 2

Pencil.
8 x 9 9/16 in.   20.2 x 24.3 cm.

56. ORNAMENTAL GATE, 1892.   FLLW/LHS No. 35

Annotations in pencil by Frank Lloyd Wright, on the left: *Louis Sullivan*, on the lower right: *Perforated gates, Bronze Doors (FLLW) to be (seen behind), FLLW. Drawn by FLLW from design by Louis H. Sullivan for gates. Tracing by FLLW from drawing by L.H.S.* These annotations partly cover and obscure: *Tracing . . . Getty Tomb* [sic] *. . . (Bronze Grille).*
Ink on linen.
27 5/8 x 23 3/4 in.   70.0 x 60.2 cm.

These drawings depict ornamental areas that were originally intended to complement each other. The first (No. 55), was conceived as an ornamental frame for the door to the tomb and the second (No. 56), as an exquisite bronze gate to fill the opening. Unfortunately, the gate, which would have been one of Sullivan's finest ornamental works, was never executed.[28]

The working drawings for the tomb are dated March 2, 1892.[29] These and three full-size drawings for the ornamental friezes of the tomb dated at the end of January 1892 (Fig. 36), and now in the collection of the College of Architecture and Design at the University of Michigan, provide an approximate time for the design of the door frame and gate. The ornaments of the Wainwright Tomb are in a transitional style connecting Sullivan's early mature organic ornament of 1890-1891 with his more geometric work of 1892-1894. The gate belongs to the earlier style, the door frame to the later.

ORNAMENTAL DESIGNS

57. ORNAMENTAL GALLERY, dated June 5, 1892.   FLLW/LHS No. 98

Inscribed: *L H S. June 5/92.*
Pencil on paper ruled lightly with pink lines and imprinted with *Adler & Sullivan, Auditorium Building Tower, Chicago . . . 189 . .*
8 3/8 x 5 3/8 in.   21.3 x 13.6 cm.

Ornamental galleries were much favored by Sullivan in 1892. Similar galleries appeared in his remodeling of Sinai Temple and his addition to the Standard Club.[30] Yet this drawing cannot be related in detail to any drawings for or photographs of these buildings and we must suppose that this was either an early study for one of these commissions, much changed in execution, or else was related to an unknown commission.

[28] Published in the *Engineering Magazine*, III (August 1892), 640.
[29] On microfilm at the Burnham Library.
[30] For an illustration of the interior of Sinai Temple see Hyman Meites, ed., *History of the Jews in Chicago* (Chicago, 1924), p. 171; for the Standard Club addition see *Inland Architect*, XXII (Nov. 1893).

Sullivan was also very fond of ornamental lions and lions' heads at this time and used them on the 1891-1892 Transportation Building (No. 53), the 1892 Union Trust Building in St. Louis, and intended to use lions' heads on his 1892 Meyer Building in Chicago.

58. ORNAMENTAL DESIGN,   FLLW/LHS No. 112
    dated November 13, 1893.

    Inscribed: *L H S. Nov. 13/93.*
    Pencil.
    3 1/4 x 5 1/2 in.   8.3 x 14.0 cm.

As both the Chicago Stock Exchange Building and the St. Nicholas Hotel in St. Louis were under construction in November 1893, it is possible this drawing was made for one of them. However, it cannot be identified with any known ornament.

59. ORNAMENTAL STUDY, dated January 31, 1894.   FLLW/LHS No. 8

    Inscribed in pencil: *Jan 31/94.* Figures in pencil at the bottom: *5778.* Annotations in pencil by Frank Lloyd Wright, in the lower right corner: *cut, #34,* and associated crop marks.
    Pencil.
    4 11/16 x 5 7/8 in.   11.9 x 14.9 cm.
    Genius, with caption: *Studies for terra cotta. 1894-95.*

Although this sketch may have been made for an Adler & Sullivan commission, its asymmetry argues against that possibility. Sullivan's designs for architectural ornament were ordinarily symmetrical except in a few cases where balance was achieved by arranging two nonsymmetrical ornaments as mirror images. And when the asymmetry of this design is coupled with its unrestrained and explosive lines, the conclusion that this is an ornamental study without particular destination seems the more reasonable. The many large leaves are unusual for this period in Sullivan's work.

CHICAGO STOCK EXCHANGE BUILDING, CHICAGO, ILLINOIS

60. ORNAMENTAL CAPITALS.   (Fig. 37)   FLLW/LHS No. 57
    dated February 1, 1894.

    Legend in pencil: *Octagon Caps. Stock Exchange Room. —like this. Regular octagons. A & S. Feb 1/94.* Notations in pencil, at bottom of capital: *Shaft of Scagliola,* on the right: *Profile, flush joint,* and dimensions.
    Pencil.
    7 15/16 x 10 in.   20.2 x 25.4 cm.

61. ORNAMENTAL ANGLE BLOCK,   FLLW/LHS No. 30
    dated March 14, 1894.

    Legend in pencil: *Chicago Stock Exchg. Bldg. Adler & Sullivan, Archts. Angle block in railing of Main Stairs. A & S. March 14/94.* Notations: *Note: Double-faced Cast-*

ing, Face 1 1/2", Same ornament on face, and in the lower right corner: *4" x 1/4" bar.*
Pencil on heavy-weight drawing paper.
18 1/4 x 22 in.   46.2 x 55.7 cm.

62. ORNAMENTAL CAPITAL, dated March 19, 1894.   FLLW/LHS No. 58

Legend in pencil: *Stock Exchg Bldg. Plaster Caps in Banking Rm. Adler & Sullivan. March 19/94.* Notations in pencil, below capital: *Flush, Plaster, Round Cor. 1 1/2" Radius,* and dimensions.
Pencil.
10 x 7 15/16 in.   25.3 x 20.2 cm.

All three drawings are elegant examples of Sullivan's geometric style, 1892-1894. The two of capitals are final sketches ready for his chief draftsman; the angle block is a full-size working drawing by Sullivan. Normally full-size drawings from Sullivan's sketches would have been made by Sullivan's chief draftsman, who at this time was George Elmslie. But, as this drawing suggests, whenever the work load grew especially heavy, Sullivan would lend his chief assistant a hand at working up his sketches. That the office was particularly busy during March 1894 is evident from the surviving drawings for the St. Nicholas Hotel, St. Louis, two of which are also dated in that month. A further contribution to the work load was the loss of Wright, whom Sullivan had fired in the famous parting of the ways in June 1893.

The plaster capitals of the Stock Exchange Room were saved when the building was demolished and are now preserved at The Art Institute of Chicago where the entire room has been rebuilt. The capitals of the banking room and the angle blocks of the stair railings were removed during early interior remodelings and do not survive.

ST. NICHOLAS HOTEL, ST. LOUIS, MISSOURI

63. ORNAMENTAL CAPITAL, dated March 10, 1894.   FLLW/LHS No. 62

Legend in pencil: *St Nicholas. Plaster Caps on Wood Cols. in Rotunda. A & S. March 10/94.* Notations in pencil, at top: *St. Nicholas,* on right side: *Plaster Cap,* below capital: *wood shaft.*
Pencil on imprinted Adler & Sullivan stationery.
8 5/16 x 5 5/16 in.   21.1 x 13.5 cm.

64. ORNAMENTAL CAPITAL, dated March 10, 1894.   FLLW/LHS No. 63

Legend in pencil: *Plaster Cap in Waiting Room. A & S. March 10/94.* Notations in pencil, at top: *St Nicholas,* above capital: *Square Abacus,* below capital: *Round, Plaster shaft, Plan of abacus.*
Pencil on imprinted Adler & Sullivan stationery.
8 5/16 x 5 5/16 in.   21.1 x 13.6 cm.

65. ORNAMENTAL FIREPLACE,   (Fig. 39)   FLLW/LHS No. 26
dated May 1894.

Legend in pencil: [St.] *Nicholas Hotel.* [St. Louis,] *Mo.* Lettered in pencil in lower right corner of the fireplace: *L. H. S. 5 '94.* Notations in pencil, on left side of fire-

place: *Mosaic, Br*[ick], *T*[erra] *C*[otta]. Annotations in pencil by Frank Lloyd Wright, at bottom: *cut, Fold, Double page, From now on degeneracy*, at sides: *cut*, at top: *cut, Fold*, and associated crop marks.
Pencil on heavy-weight drawing paper.
13 1/2 x 19 1/2 in.   34.2 x 49.3 cm.
Genius, with caption: *Brick and terra cotta fireplace. St. Nicholas Hotel, St. Louis. 1893-94.*

66. ORNAMENTAL CAPITAL, dated June 23, 1894.   FLLW/LHS No. 41

Legend in pencil: *St Nicholas Hotel. Caps of Cols in Bar Room. 6. 23. 94. AS & R.* Notation in pencil left of capital: *Development of Pattern*, and below capital: *Shaft, Ceiling.*
Pencil on imprinted Adler & Sullivan stationery.
8 1/16 x 5 5/16 in.   20.5 x 13.4 cm.
Genius, with caption: *Column cap in terra cotta. St. Nicholas Hotel, St. Louis. 1893-94.*

67. ORNAMENTAL STENCILS, dated July 27, 1894.   FLLW/LHS No. 69

Legend in pencil: *St Nicholas Hotel. AS & R. July 27/94.* Notations in pencil, upper left: *Gentlemens Restaurant*, at top: *Restaurant*, upper center: *Café*, at left and in center, not in Sullivan's hand: *(Drawn full size)*.
Pencil.
8 3/16 x 10 7/8 in.   20.8 x 27.5 cm.

68. ORNAMENTAL STENCIL, dated July 28, 1894.   FLLW/LHS No. 60

Legend in pencil: *St Nicholas Hotel. July 28/94. AS & R.* Notation in pencil, not in Sullivan's hand: *(Drawn full size)*. There is an erasure between the two lines of the legend that seems to read: *12" stencil border for color decoration.*
Pencil.
4 11/16 x 4 1/2 in.   11.9 x 11.5 cm.

69. ORNAMENTAL STENCIL, dated July 28, 1894.   FLLW/LHS No. 70

Legend in pencil: *St Nicholas. 12" Color-border stencil. AS & R. July 28/94.* Notation in pencil, not in Sullivan's hand: *(Drawn full size)*.
Pencil.
4 3/4 x 5 3/8 in.   12.1 x 13.7 cm.

70. ORNAMENTAL STENCIL, dated July 28, 1894.   FLLW/LHS No. 71

Legend in pencil: *Stencils for Color decoration. A & S & R. July 28/94.* Notation in pencil, not in Sullivan's hand: *(Drawn full size)*.
Pencil.
4 7/8 x 5 1/2 in.   12.4 x 13.9 cm.

71. ORNAMENTAL STENCILS, dated July 28, 1894.   FLLW/LHS No. 67

Legend in pencil: *St Nicholas Hotel, St Louis. AS & R. July 28/1894.* Notations in pencil above and right of lower design: *12" Border.*

Pencil.
10 7/8 x 8 1/4 in.   27.6 x 20.9 cm.

72. ORNAMENTAL STENCIL,   (Fig. 38)   FLLW/LHS No. 65
dated July 31, 1894.

Legend in pencil: *St Nicholas. Stencil Border 12". July 31/94. Banquet Hall Ceiling.*
Notation in pencil, not in Sullivan's hand: *(Drawn Full size).*
Pencil.
7 7/8 x 8 3/16 in.   20.1 x 20.8 cm.

73. ORNAMENTAL STENCILS, dated August 10, 1894.   FLLW/LHS No. 68

Legend in pencil: *St Nicholas Hotel. Pattern for Color Stencil. AS & R. Aug 10/94.*
Notations in pencil below upper design: *Soffit of beams in Gentlemen's Restaurant,*
and to right of lower design: *Border in Ceiling of Entrance Vestibule.* Notations in
pencil, not in Sullivan's hand, right of upper design and below lower design: *(Drawn
full size).*
Pencil.
10 7/8 x 8 1/4 in.   27.5 x 20.6 cm.

74. ORNAMENTAL STENCILS, dated August 18, 1894.   FLLW/LHS No. 72

Legend in pencil: *St Nicholas Hotel. Diaper for walls of Rotunda. AS & R. Aug
13/94.* Notation in pencil near bottom right: *C[enter] line.* Notation in pencil, not in
Sullivan's hand, at bottom right: *(Drawn full size).*
Pencil.
3 7/8 x 6 1/2 in.   9.9 x 16.5 cm.

75. ORNAMENTAL STENCIL,   FLLW/LHS No. 66
dated September 20, 1894.

Legend in pencil: *St Nicholas Hotel. 12" Border in Ceiling. Gentlemens Restaurant.
Sept 20/94.*
Pencil.
6 9/16 x 8 1/4 in.   16.7 x 20.9 cm.

76. ORNAMENTAL STENCILS, 1894.   FLLW/LHS No. 61

Legend in pencil: *St Nicholas. Stencil for Waiting Room Wall.* Notations in pencil,
at top: *6" border above picture moulding,* at lower right: *Every 2 ft center,* and in center, not in Sullivan's hand: *(both drawn full size).*
Pencil.
5 9/16 x 8 1/4 in.   14.1 x 20.9 cm.

The many drawings for the St. Nicholas Hotel are instructive in several ways. The
six-month time span between the first and last of them gives us some idea of how very
long Sullivan sometimes had to work to complete the interior decoration of a large ornamental building like the St. Nicholas. The drawings also confirm what one might suppose
about the sequence in which the ornamental drawings were made: the plaster ornaments,
which needed to be modeled, molded, and set in place before the interior painting could
begin, were designed before the stencils.

One of the most interesting drawings in the series shows the magnificent fifteen-foot wide fireplace (No. 65) of the Banquet Hall on the top floor of the hotel (Figs. 38-39). In contrast to all the other drawings for hotel decorations, this is a working drawing made personally by Sullivan. While much of the extemporaneous quality of Sullivan's smaller sketches is lost in this work, the skilled bravura of the master remains, as is obvious whenever this drawing is compared to similar drawings by Sullivan's draftsmen (Nos. 31, 39, 117-18, 120-22).

The drawing is unusual and problematical to a degree because of the decorations in the lunette immediately over the fireplace, which are not in Sullivan's geometric style of 1892-1894. These rounded organic motifs supporting widespreading leafy branches anticipate Sullivan's next ornamental style, which appeared in earnest the following year, 1895. Evidently Wright also looked on the drawing as the prelude to a stylistic change in Sullivan's ornament, one that seemed to forecast a decline in Sullivan's ornamental prowess, for he scribbled unceremoniously across the drawing, "From now on degeneracy."

Sullivan continued to make designs for the stencil decorations in the hotel during July, August, and September 1895. These diminutive drawings, among the most exquisite he ever made, exhibit a rapid and sure control of the pencil despite their small size and considerable complexity. Four of them, in fact, were made on the same day, July 28, 1894 (Nos. 68-71). One of the finest (No. 72), used on the ceiling of the Banquet Hall, served as an elegant counterpart to Sullivan's great fireplace at the end of the room (Fig. 38).

Nearly all of Sullivan's designs for stencils carry the notation "(Drawn full size)." As sketches of this type would ordinarily have been enlarged to full size, one wonders why this special note was necessary. The answer may lie in the notations themselves, which are not in the handwriting of either Sullivan or his chief draftsman, George Elmslie, and may therefore have been added by someone outside the Adler & Sullivan office. If so, the notations can most reasonably be attributed to the decorating firm of Healy & Millet, which as contractor for painting the stencils may well have enlarged Sullivan's sketches to suit its special requirements. That these sketches were somehow handled outside the usual Adler & Sullivan office routine is also implied by the survival of so many of them.

The notation "AS & R" on so many of the drawings is Sullivan's abbreviation for Adler & Sullivan and Ramsey, the latter being Charles Ramsey, a St. Louis architect with whom Adler & Sullivan associated whenever they had a commission in that city.

TAYLOR BUILDING REMODELING, CHICAGO, ILLINOIS

77. ORNAMENTAL ELEVATOR SCREEN,   FLLW/LHS No. 12
dated July 10, 1894.

Legend in pencil: *Taylor Bldg. Elevator Screen. Scale 1/8" = 1 foot. 7.10.94.* Notations in pencil, on the left, upper band: *moulding . . . lapped,* lower band: *face.*
Pencil.
5 3/8 x 8 1/4 in. 13.7 x 20.9 cm.

78. ORNAMENTAL ELEVATOR SCREEN,   FLLW/LHS No. 59
dated July 27, 1894.

Legend in pencil: *Taylor Bldg. A & S. July 27/94.* Notations in pencil on the upper left: *Perforated, Single faced Casting,* at the top: *3/8" x 3/4" Bars,* center top: *2 wires crimped, Straight wires, woven wire mesh,* and in the lower right: *Elevator Veil in Elevator Enclosure.*
Pencil on imprinted Adler & Sullivan stationery.
5 1/4 x 8 3/8 in.   13.4 x 21.2 cm.

A building by this name, built shortly after the fire of 1871, was razed in 1911 to make way for the Harris Trust Building at 111-19 West Monroe Street in Chicago.[31] The six-story post-fire Taylor Building had probably been built without an elevator; and by 1894, with an economic depression at hand, the owners may finally have recognized, however reluctantly, the necessity for installing one. Ordinarily Adler & Sullivan would have avoided or refused such a relatively unrewarding commission. But perhaps in this case they were inclined to accept it because of a personal friendship with the owner or because of a genuine need for commissions, regardless of size, during the depression that had begun the previous year.

ELIEL APARTMENT BUILDING PROJECT, CHICAGO, ILLINOIS

79. ELIEL APARTMENT BUILDING,   FLLW/LHS No. 23
dated November 28, 1894.

Legend in pencil: *Eliel – 50 ft 11 stories. Nov. 28/94. A & S.* Notations in pencil, building width: *50 ft.,* height: *130.0* [ft.], on slope of roof: *30'.*
Pencil on imprinted Adler & Sullivan stationery.
10 13/16 x 7 7/8 in.   27.4 x 20.0 cm.

In this elevation we are treated to a rare glimpse of Sullivan's architectural imagination conjuring up, with apparently the same ease and facility that marks his ornamental sketches, the vision of an elegantly proportioned and highly ornamental building in its entirety. The building was probably intended as an investment for Adler's friend Levy A. Eliel, but the scheme was not destined to be carried out because of the depressed economic conditions in the 1890's. Its height, exactly one hundred and thirty feet, reflects a municipal ordinance enacted by the City of Chicago in the early 1890's restricting the height of tall buildings to that level.[32]

ORNAMENTAL DESIGNS

80. ORNAMENTAL DESIGNS, about 1894.   FLLW/LHS No. 81

Pencil on tracing paper.
8 3/16 x 6 3/4 in.   20.8 x 17.1 cm.

[31] Frank A. Randall, *History of the Development of Building Construction in Chicago* (Urbana, 1949), p. 238.

[32] An ordinance limiting the height of buildings in Chicago to 130 feet was passed by the City Council on March 13, 1893.

81. ORNAMENTAL DESIGN, about 1894.   FLLW/LHS No. 96
    Pencil.
    10 11/16 x 8 5/16 in.   27.0 x 21.2 cm.

82. ORNAMENTAL DESIGN, about 1894.   FLLW/LHS No. 108
    Pencil.
    3 1/8 x 1 15/16 in.   7.9 x 5.0 cm.

83. ORNAMENTAL DESIGN, about 1894.   FLLW/LHS No. 109
    Pencil.
    3 3/8 x 2 3/16 in.   8.5 x 5.6 cm.
    Drawings Nos. 82 and 83 may have been cut from the same piece of paper.

84. ORNAMENTAL DESIGN, about 1894.   FLLW/LHS No. 107
    Pencil.
    3 1/8 x 3 5/16 in.   7.9 x 8.4 cm.

85. ORNAMENTAL DESIGN, about 1894.   FLLW/LHS No. 113
    Pencil.
    2 3/8 x 4 3/8 in.   6.0 x 11.1 cm.

These drawings, without dates or inscriptions, belong stylistically to Sullivan's geometric ornament of 1892-1894. They are perhaps best assigned to the year 1894 because of their similarities to Sullivan's drawings for the St. Nicholas Hotel: No. 80 should be compared with No. 75, No. 81 with No. 66, and No. 82 with No. 73. Although the other three drawings (Nos. 83-85) cannot be related so directly to the designs for the St. Nicholas Hotel, they are nevertheless sufficiently like other drawings of 1894 to warrant inclusion in the group.

HAIR ORNAMENTS

86. HAIRPIN, dated August 21, 1894.   FLLW/LHS No. 110
    Legend in pencil: *Ladies Hair Pin (for . . . [illegible]). Aug 21/94.*
    Pencil.
    6 3/16 x 5 3/16 in.   15.7 x 13.3 cm.

87. COMB, dated January 4, 1895.   FLLW/LHS No. 99
    Legend in pencil: *Ladies Comb (for back hair). Jan 4/95.* Sullivan's monogram. Notations in pencil, at top: *Center line,* on right from top to bottom: *Rubies, open, Carved gold (double band), Lapis Lazuli, diamond, line of the hair.*
    Pencil.
    10 1/2 x 8 9/16 in.   26.6 x 21.7 cm.

88. HAIRPINS, dated January 31, 1895.   FLLW/LHS No. 111
    Legend in pencil: *Hair pin. LHS. Jan 31/95.*
    Pencil.
    5 7/16 x 3 in.   13.8 x 7.7 cm.

89. COMB, dated June 29, 1895.   FLLW/LHS No. 44

Inscribed in pencil: *Comb. June 29/95.*
Pencil.
4 1/4 x 5 1/2 in.   10.8 x 13.0 cm.
Genius, with caption: *Carved amber comb. 1895.*

During the ten months from August 21, 1894, to June 29, 1895, Sullivan made four designs for hair ornaments. Nothing at all is known about the persons commissioning them or their present whereabouts, if indeed they were ever made. Their style is transitional between Sullivan's geometric work of 1892-1894 and his more organic ornaments of the second half of the 1890's. In the drawing of August 1894 (No. 86), there are hints of the rounded organic forms that would increase in number and significance in Sullivan's ornamental work during and after 1895. Broad curvilinear organic shapes of this character also occur in the upper part of the comb designed January 4, 1895 (No. 87). In the other comb of June 29, 1895 (No. 89), one of the new triangular motifs with inward curving sides serves as the dominant shape. It is not known why in *Genius* Wright refers to No. 89 as a "carved amber comb."

ORATORY MEDAL

90. MEDAL DESIGN,   (Figs. 41-42)   FLLW/LHS No. 55
dated January 29, 1895.

Inscribed in pencil on the medal: *Awarded to Robert McMurdy for excellence in ORATORY, University of Michigan, 1895,* and in the lower right corner: *Jan 29/95.*
Pencil.
3 3/16 x 7 3/16 in.   8.1 x 18.2 cm.

91. MEDAL DESIGN,   (Fig. 42)   FLLW/LHS No. 56
dated January 30, 1895.

Inscribed in pencil: *Actual size 2 1/2" diam. L.H.S. Jan 30/95.*
Pencil.
10 3/4 x 8 7/16 in.   27.2 x 21.5 cm.

In January 1895, Sullivan was approached by Robert McMurdy and I. Giles Lewis with a commission from the Alumni Association of the University of Michigan for a medal to be presented to the winner of the annual competition sponsored by the Northern Oratorical League.[33] Sullivan accepted and began with a generalized study of each side at full scale on a single piece of paper (No. 90). On the following day he presumably made two drawings, one of each side, at approximately twice the intended final size of two and one-half inches. Of the two, only the drawing for the reverse side survives in the Avery collection (No. 91).

According to a newspaper clipping,[34] the task of reproducing Sullivan's design proved

[33] The commission probably came to Sullivan through Lewis, who must have been a close friend of the architect as he later served as a witness at Sullivan's marriage in 1899.

[34] *Chicago Tribune*, June 14, 1896, p. 9. I am indebted to Tim Samuelson for this reference. See also Edward J. Vaughn, "Sullivan and Elmslie at Michigan," *Prairie School Review*, VI (Second Quarter, 1969), 21-23.

so difficult that it was not until Charles E. Barber, Chief Engraver of the United States Mint at Philadelphia, offered his services that the design was successfully engraved. From his dies twenty-five medals were struck in bronze. One of them, now in the Avery Library, was Sullivan's personal copy. Before being presented to Sullivan, it was cut in half so that both sides could be viewed simultaneously (Figs. 41-42).

It is instructive to compare Sullivan's first study for the medal with his detailed working out. Although generally adhering to the original inspiration, Sullivan did not hesitate to change proportions and details. An even more interesting comparison may be made between the final drawing and the medal itself, on which the details were considerably simplified because of the difficulties encountered in engraving. This is especially noticeable in the leafy passages and the areas of linear spirals. As Sullivan's designs were ordinarily intended for much larger decorations normally carried out by modeling and casting rather than by stamping, the results were usually closer to the original than here. Nonetheless, there were always some modifications, and the differences exhibited between drawing and medal serve to remind us that when investigating Sullivan's ornament it is important, wherever possible, to refer to both the ornament and the drawing for it.

ORNAMENTAL TITLE PAGE

92. TITLE PAGE DESIGN, dated March 5, 1895.   FLLW/LHS No. 85

Lettering in pencil: *INSPIRATION*. Sullivan's monogram. *3 - 5 - 95*.
Pencil on medium-weight drawing paper.
5 3/8 x 8 in. 13.7 x 20.3 cm.

93. TITLE PAGE DESIGN, about March 1895.   FLLW/LHS No. 16

Lettering in pencil: *INSPIRATION. A POEM IN PROSE. Louis H. Sullivan. 1886.*
Pencil on tracing paper.
8 5/8 x 13 5/8 in. 21.9 x 34.5 cm.

Sullivan's poem "Inspiration" remained a constant preoccupation of his throughout his life. He had written the poem in 1886 and read it before the third annual convention of the Western Association of Architects in Chicago on November 17 of that year.[35] In a letter to Walt Whitman of February 2, 1887, Sullivan enclosed a copy of the poem with these words, "At the time I met your work I was engaged upon the essay I herewith send you. I had just finished Decadence."[36] Sullivan's concern for poetic expression together with his love of the poetry of Whitman and the music of Wagner are characteristic of the romantic side of Sullivan's genius.

A drawing of about 1887 called "Spring Song—a decoration" was an early example of Sullivan's desire to translate the poem into graphic form.[37] Another drawing published by David Gebhard and attributed by him to George Elmslie, who remained Sullivan's chief draftsman until 1909, is also in Sullivan's hand and should probably be asso-

---

[35] Published in the *Inland Architect*, VIII (December 1886), 61-64.

[36] As quoted by Sherman Paul, *Louis Sullivan* (New York, 1962), p. 2, from Horace Traubel, *With Walt Whitman in Camden* (New York, 1914), III, pp. 25-26.

[37] Illustrated in the *Chicago Architectural Club Annual*, 1902.

ciated with the two drawings of 1895.[38] No doubt Sullivan made them all as part of a scheme to publish his poem, but the project must have fallen through as no record of the publication has been discovered. In 1899 Sullivan combined "Inspiration" with two other poems, "The Master" and "Sympathy—a Romanza," under the comprehensive title of "Nature and the Poet" but again, whatever hopes he may have had for publication of the extended poem were not realized.[39]

It is with these drawings and others of early 1895 (Nos. 87-93) that Sullivan's ornamental style of the latter half of the 1890's appeared in its fully developed form. From then on Sullivan sought to achieve a balance between organic and geometric motifs. Organic areas were mostly leafy patches applied to broad, gently curving stems or to spiraling motifs that were half naturalistic and half geometric. His geometric motifs consisted of rectangles, triangles, and polygons with inward curving sides alternated with smaller areas of interpenetrating geometric designs. Because of the few drawings by Sullivan surviving from the early years of the twentieth century, it is not possible to determine precisely when his style of the late 1890's gave way to the style of his last years.

GUARANTY BUILDING, BUFFALO, NEW YORK

94. ORNAMENTAL STAIR RAILING, (Fig. 43)   FLLW/LHS No. 73
dated June 18, 1895.

Legend in pencil: *Guaranty Bldg, Buffalo. Sketch for Stair Railing in Cast Iron. June 18/95.*
Pencil on imprinted Adler & Sullivan stationery.
7 15/16 x 5 3/8 in.   20.2 x 13.6 cm.

95. ORNAMENTAL FASCIA, dated June 24, 1895.   FLLW/LHS No. 74

Legend in pencil: *Facia of Stair well. Guaranty Bldg, Buffalo. Adler & Sullivan, archts. June 24/95.* Notations in pencil, on the right: *Plaster ceiling*, and in the center toward the bottom: *not used.*
Pencil.
11 7/8 x 8 3/8 in.   27.5 x 21.2 cm.

96. ORNAMENTAL PIER, (Fig. 44)   FLLW/LHS No. 48
dated July 13, 1895.

Legend in pencil: *Decoration of Col. at Stairway.* Sullivan's monogram. *July 13–95. Scale 3″ = 1 foot. Adler & Sullivan Archts.* [Guaranty] *Building, Buffalo, N.Y.* Notations in pencil, right side: *10.6 4.5.6.7.8.9.10.11.12. stories. 11.6 2.3 stories*, right top: *Facia* [?] *2 1/2 wide*, bottom right: *Floor line*, and dimensions. Annotations in pencil by Frank Lloyd Wright, at bottom: *cut*, and associated crop marks.
Pencil.
11 3/4 x 8 in.   29.8 x 20.3 cm.

[38] David Gebhard, *Drawings for Architectural Ornament by George Grant Elmslie*, (Santa Barbara, 1968), pl. 1; see also W. R. Hasbrouck, "Elmslie Drawings," *Prairie School Review*, VI (Third Quarter, 1969), 27.
[39] A copy is in the Burnham Library.

Genius, with caption: *Terra cotta pier*. [Wright is contrasting the drawing with another (No. 40) for an ornamental soffit in McVicker's Theater] *Drawing shows change in method. Guarantee [sic] Building, Buffalo. 1895.*
The pier as executed is cast iron.

97. ORNAMENTAL DOORPLATE,   (Fig. 45)   FLLW/LHS No. 124
dated July 18, 1895.

Legend in pencil: *Sketch Study. Guaranty Bldg, Buffalo. Hardware. A & S. July. 18–95. L. H. S.* Notations in pencil on the design, from top to bottom: *Lock barrel, Stem of Knob.*
Pencil.
13 x 7 15/16 in.   32.9 x 20.1 cm.

98. ORNAMENTAL CAPITAL,   (Fig. 46)   FLLW/LHS No. 75
dated August 21, 1895.

Legend in pencil: *Guaranty Bldg. Capital 1st Story Cols.* Sullivan's monogram. *Aug 21/95.* Notations in pencil, in medallion: *Guaranty,* and dimensions.
Pencil on imprinted Adler & Sullivan stationery.
11 13/16 x 7 7/8 in.   27.5 x 20.0 cm.

99. ORNAMENTAL CAPITAL,   (Fig. 46)   FLLW/LHS No. 76
dated August 23, 1895.

Legend in pencil: *Guaranty Building, Buffalo. Adler & Sullivan, Architects. Terra Cotta Capital. First story Columns.* Sullivan's monogram. *Aug. 23ᵈ 1895. Finis.* Notations in pencil, on shaft: *Bands 2" each,* and dimensions.
Pencil.
8 3/8 x 11 1/2 in.   21.3 x 29.2 cm.

The surviving drawings for ornamental details of the Guaranty Building are dated June 18 through August 23, 1895, just before and after the Adler & Sullivan partnership was terminated. Adler began work as consultant to the Crane Elevator Co. on July 11, 1895, leaving Sullivan with little more than two commissions besides the Guaranty Building: a remodeling and addition to the Burnet Hotel in Cincinnati and a tall building for St. Louis, neither of which was ever carried out.

All of the Guaranty drawings, except one, are for ornamental details which can still be identified in the building. The exception (No. 95) is for the facia of the stair well, which as the notation on the drawing tells us was not used. These ornamental details all belong to Sullivan's style of the second half of the 1890's.

The most puzzling drawings in the Guaranty group are the two for the exterior ground floor capitals (Nos. 98-99). Even though construction of the building would logically have proceeded from outside to inside, these drawings for exterior ornaments are dated after the ones for interior decorations. Since it is highly unlikely that Sullivan ordinarily designed interior appointments before finishing the exterior ornamentation of his buildings, we must suppose that in this case a problem arose necessitating the redesign of these capitals at the last minute.

Sullivan's drawing for an interior pier (No. 96) is also of special interest because it is a scaled working drawing. In his book, *Louis Sullivan*, Hugh Morrison remarks that Sullivan personally detailed the interior ornament and the column capitals, but offers no further explanation.[40] If by "detailed," Morrison meant that Sullivan made working drawings, then this drawing for an interior pier helps confirm his statement. And if Sullivan did in fact make other working drawings for the interior ornamentation of the Guaranty Building, he probably made them more through necessity than by choice in order to assist his staff, which must have been harder pressed than usual because of the loss of Adler.

ORNAMENTAL FRAME

100. *INLAND ARCHITECT*: (Fig. 47)   FLLW/LHS No. 123
ORNAMENTAL FRAME FOR HUNT
MEMORIAL PAGE, dated August 3, 1895.

Legend in pencil: *Hunt Frame. Aug 3–95*. Sullivan's monogram. Notations in pencil, on the right: *Center Line*, in the lower right corner: *HUNT*.
Pencil.
6 11/16 x 8 in.   17.0 x 20.3 cm.

To memorialize the architect Richard Morris Hunt, who died July 31, 1895, the editor of *Inland Architect* asked Sullivan to design a commemorative page. On August 3 Sullivan made this sketch and on August 7 he finished the design, which was published in the August 1895 issue of *Inland Architect*. (Fig. 47)[41] Curiously Sullivan's sketch bears absolutely no relationship to the published design. Considering that only four days separated the unused sketch and the finished design, one wonders how Sullivan found time to start over again and complete an entirely new design while he was personally in charge of a large office in the midst of getting out ornamental drawings for the Guaranty Building.

The answer may lie in the ornament at the bottom and sides of Hunt's portrait which seems to be in Sullivan's style of the Auditorium and Banquet Hall periods (1888-1891) while the ornament above his head, on the other hand, is in Sullivan's style of 1895. It may be that the heavy pressure Sullivan was under after Adler left the office made it impossible for him to finish the study of August 3 in time for publication. Sullivan may, therefore, have decided to adapt an earlier drawing in order to meet the deadline of the magazine. If he did so, it is the parts below and at the sides of Hunt's portrait that he traced from the earlier drawing. To complete the frame he needed only to add—in his somewhat different current style—the lettering and details in the triangular fields above Hunt's head.

That Sullivan produced the page in this manner is supported by his later reworking of the Hunt page for the frontispiece of the 1902 Chicago Architectural Club Annual. There Sullivan substituted a long poetic inscription for Hunt's portrait and added, "C. A. C.," and the year, "1902."

[40] *Louis Sullivan*, p. 174.
[41] Published in the *Inland Architect*, XXVI (August 1895). Sullivan's copy of the page with the inscribed date is in the Burnham Library.

ORNAMENTAL DESIGN

101. ORNAMENTAL DESIGN, dated August 12, 1895.   FLLW/LHS No. 10

Inscribed in pencil: *Aug 12/95*. Annotations in pencil by Frank Lloyd Wright, at the top and bottom: *cut*, and associated crop marks.
Pencil.
6 7/8 x 5 1/2 in.   17.4 x 13.9 cm.
Genius, with caption: *Studies for terra cotta. 1894-95*.

Although the date of August 12, 1895, suggests that this drawing may have been made for the Guaranty Building, there is no ornament in the building that corresponds to it. If it was designed for the building, it must have been intended for some unusual place as Sullivan's designs for ornament were nearly always symmetrical. There is no indication on the drawing that it was intended for execution in terra cotta.

ORNAMENTAL LETTERS

102. ORNAMENTAL LETTER S,   FLLW/LHS No. 103
dated August 31, 1895.

Inscribed in pencil: *Aug 31–95*.
Pencil.
2 11/16 x 2 9/16 in.   6.8 x 6.5 cm.

103. ORNAMENTAL LETTER K,   FLLW/LHS No. 105
dated May 21, 1896.

Inscribed in pencil: *5–21–96*. Notation in ink: *6000.–*
Pencil.
3 x 2 13/16 in.   7.7 x 7.1 cm.

104. ORNAMENTAL LETTER B,   FLLW/LHS No. 104
dated June 25, 1896.

Inscribed in pencil: *6.25.96*.
Pencil.
2 1/4 x 3 in.   5.7 x 7.6 cm.

These drawings for ornamental letters do not correspond to the requirements of any known architectural commission of 1895-1896. Although they are clearly related to each other stylistically, the relatively long time span between the first and last makes it doubtful that they belonged to a single project.

MUSIC COVER

105. ORNAMENTAL COVER FOR   (Fig. 48)   FLLW/LHS No. 84
MUSIC, dated November 27, 1896.

Inscribed in pencil: *LHS. Nov 27–'96*. Lettering and writing in pencil as part of the design, top to bottom: *MUSIC. D. F. . . . [illegible]. A monthly Magazine. P. . . . 1896. W.S.B. Matthews, Editor*.

Pencil on the back of a Chicago Athletic Association restaurant check.
6 1/4 x 4 7/16 in.   15.7 x 11.2 cm.

Presumably W.S.B. Matthews, editor of *Music*, had decided to improve his journal with a more artistic cover and asked Sullivan for a design during lunch at the Chicago Athletic Club on November 27, 1896. No doubt Sullivan with his longstanding musical interests, was already well-known to Matthews. Apparently Sullivan's response was to call for a restaurant check on the back of which he quickly sketched his idea for the cover.

Holding to the essentials of this sketch as he had been taught to do at the École des Beaux-Arts in Paris, Sullivan elaborated and refined the design. The result was a handsome and especially good example of Sullivan's decorative style of the second half of the 1890's (Fig. 48). Unfortunately Matthews altered Sullivan's design after it had appeared in a few issues of the magazine evidently because Sullivan's elegant lettering did not read well. In its place he substituted heavily shaded letters on a field of angular motifs completely out of character with the rest of the design.

COUNTRY CLUB PROJECT

106. DRAWING OF A COUNTRY CLUB,   FLLW/LHS No. 116
dated June 26, 1898.

Legend in pencil: *Country Club. 6–26–98.* Sullivan's monogram. Notations in pencil, at the bottom: *Open 4 sides,* upper right: *Plan.*
Pencil on the back of a business card.
2 1/4 x 3 7/16 in.   5.7 x 8.7 cm.
Reverse: *Louis H. Sullivan, Architect. 1600 Auditorium Tower, Chicago.*

This is a particularly fine example of Sullivan's ability to conjure up, on what was surely the spur of the moment, an architectural design that would serve him as the *esquisse* for a project. It also is unusual for its size as it is sketched with a controlled yet clairvoyant line on the back of Sullivan's business card (2 x 3 inches). Within these miniscule dimensions Sullivan provided all the essentials of the scheme: plan, elevation, legends, date, and monogram signature. Had the client decided to build the country club, there can be little question that Sullivan could have held to this original sketch in its essentials.

ORNAMENTAL DESIGNS

107. ORNAMENTAL DESIGN, dated September 12, 1898.   FLLW/LHS No. 120

Inscribed in pencil: *Sept 12–98.*
Pencil.
8 3/8 x 5 7/16 in.   21.2 x 13.8 cm.

108. ORNAMENTAL FENCE, dated September 16, 1898.   FLLW/LHS No. 95

Legend in pencil: *C.[ast] I.[ron] Fence. Sept–16–98.*
Pencil.
8 1/2 x 4 15/16 in.   21.6 x 12.5 cm.

109. ORNAMENTAL FENCE, dated January 2, 1899. FLLW/LHS No. 86

Legend in ink: *C*.[ast] *I*[ron] *Fence. 1.2–99. LHS.*
Ink.
8 3/8 x 5 3/8 in. 21.2 x 13.7 cm.

110. ORNAMENTAL FENCE, dated January 2, 1899. FLLW/LHS No. 87

Legend in ink: *Iron Fence. Jan 2–99. LHS.*
Ink.
8 3/8 x 5 3/8 in. 21.2 x 13.7 cm.

111. ORNAMENTAL DESIGN, dated January 10, 1899. FLLW/LHS No. 106

Inscribed in pencil: *Jan 10–99.*
Pencil on the back of a piece of accounting paper with a two-cent stamp affixed to it.
3 5/8 x 3 in. 9.2 x 7.7 cm.

112. ORNAMENTAL DESIGN, dated January 26, 1899. FLLW/LHS No. 115

Inscribed in pencil: *1.26.99.*
Pencil.
4 7/8 x 6 in. 12.4 x 15.3 cm.

These drawings cannot be associated with any known commission in Sullivan's office during the five-month period in which they were made. As Sullivan was working during these months on two important ornamental buildings for the Gage Brothers and Schlesinger & Mayer, it is likely that these drawings were related in some way to them but, if so, the ornaments for which they were made have not been identified.

Sullivan's two pen-and-ink drawings for a cast iron fence (Nos. 109-110) are the only surviving ornamental sketches by Sullivan in that medium. In fact, Sullivan almost never worked in ink. Even his early pen-and-ink drawings for frescoes were traced from pencil sketches (Nos. 4-8). As these sketches for a cast iron fence do not seem to be tracings, it is difficult to understand why in making them Sullivan chose to express himself in the unusual medium of pen-and-ink instead of his ubiquitous pencil.[42]

These six drawings were stolen from the Avery Library and have not yet been recovered.

GAGE BUILDING [?], CHICAGO, ILLINOIS

113. ORNAMENTAL LUNETTE, about 1899. FLLW/LHS No. 97

Pencil on heavy-weight drawing paper.
6 5/8 x 7 1/8 in. 16.8 x 18.2 cm.

This unsigned and undated work appears to be a scale drawing in Sullivan's hand for an entrance lunette of the type used on the Guaranty, Bayard, and Gage Buildings. Among these three buildings, the entrance depicted in this drawing relates most closely

[42] Presumably Sullivan's ink sketches on tracing paper of caricatures that appeared in the French magazine *Le Journal Amusant* in 1875-1876 were drawn freehand, because they are not the same size as the originals.

to the original entrance of the Gage Building, especially as regards the very similar ornaments along the perimeter of each lunette. On the other hand, as the details in the Gage lunette are quite different from those of the drawing, it is apparent that if the drawing was prepared for the Gage entrance, its details were considerably altered before execution.

This drawing was stolen from the Avery Library and has not yet been recovered.

SCHLESINGER & MAYER BUILDING, CHICAGO, ILLINOIS

114. ORNAMENTAL IRON SPANDREL, (Fig. 49)   FLLW/LHS No. 100
1899.

Notation in pencil on right: *LUXFE*[R].
Pencil on heavy-weight drawing paper.
6 1/16 x 7 3/4 in.   15.4 x 19.7 cm.

This carefully prepared working drawing for an ornamental panel on the Madison Street front of the Schlesinger & Mayer Building (now Carson Pirie Scott) is unique. Although in Sullivan's hand, as the delicately controlled and subtly manipulated lines of the pencil testify, it is highly unusual in being a scale drawing containing among other things, window frames, prismatic glass (Luxfer Prisms), and lettering. Drawings of a similar character, but by Sullivan's chief draftsman, George Elmslie, are not uncommon. A number survive from the National Farmers' Bank at Owatonna, Minn. (Nos. 116-17, 119-21), as do others by Elmslie from the years after 1909 when he was in independent practice.[43] That this drawing is, however, by Sullivan and not by Elmslie or another draftsman, is confirmed not only by its technical characteristics but also by the visual qualities of the ornamental spandrel executed from this design (Fig. 49). Of the many decorated areas on the Madison Street front, only this panel contains ornament of such distinctively high quality that it can without question be considered the personal work of Sullivan, from study sketch through working drawings. All other decorated areas of the building reflect in varying degrees the eye and hand of George Elmslie.[44] No doubt Sullivan was forced to give his personal attention to this working drawing in order to assist his small staff, which was faced with an unusually heavy work load during the summer and fall of 1899, because of the Gage and Schlesinger & Mayer commissions.

This drawing was stolen from the Avery Library and has not yet been recovered.

ORNAMENTAL DESIGN

115. ORNAMENTAL DESIGN, dated April 2, 1902.   FLLW/LHS No. 102

Inscribed in pencil: *April 2–1902. LHS.*
Pencil.
3 13/16 x 5 5/16 in.   9.7 x 13.5 cm.

[43] See Gebhard, *Drawings by George Elmslie.*
[44] For a detailed consideration of Elmslie's role in Sullivan's ornament see Paul E. Sprague, "The Ar- chitectural Ornament of Louis Sullivan" (Ph.D. Diss., Princeton University, 1968).

Although the date of this drawing seems to read April 2, 1902, it is difficult to relate its tight geometry to Sullivan's style of the late 1890's and equally hard to explain it in terms of his last ornamental style (Figs. 60-63). Only the overlapping rectangles with inward curving sides, motifs especially common in Sullivan's work during the late 1890's, suggest that the drawing continues his style of those years. But even though the drawing is thus related, however inconclusively, to the ornaments of 1895-1900, it remains sufficiently atypical of Sullivan's style during those years to serve as an example and guide to Sullivan's style during the first decade of the new century. Its subject may be an ornamental frame for a lighting fixture or, because of its resemblance to the drawings for stencils in the St. Nicholas Hotel (Nos. 67-76), the pattern for a stencil.

THE NATIONAL FARMERS' BANK, OWATONNA, MINNESOTA

116. ORNAMENTAL PANEL   FLLW/LHS Nos. 78 and 101
dated March 5, 1907.

Legend lettered in pencil: *Sketch of stone carving over shop doors and office ent. (see Broadway Elevation). National Farmers Bank of Owatonna. Louis H. Sullivan Architect. March 5/08.* Notations in pencil, at the top: *Brick*, on the left: *Joint*, in the lower left: *Scale 1 1/2 in = 1 foot*, and dimensions.
Pencil.
8 7/8 x 11 13/16 in.   22.5 x 30.0 cm.
Drawn by George Elmslie.

117. ORNAMENTAL CORNICE,   (Fig. 51)   FLLW/LHS No. 80
dated March 22, 1907.

Legend lettered in pencil: *1 1/2" Scale Detail of Cornice. Owatonna Bank. L. H. Sullivan Archt. March 22/07.* Notations in pencil on the right from top to bottom: *Dentil, 3" plain, Terra cotta, Brick, Terra Cotta, Brick*, in red pencil above dentils: *R1*, in the upper terra cotta band: *I1*, in the lower terra cotta band: *H1*, in the lunette: *G1*, and dimensions.
Pencil.
11 7/8 x 7 7/8 in.   30.0 x 20.0 cm.
Drawn by George Elmslie.

118. ORNAMENTAL COPING,   FLLW/LHS No. 1
dated March 27, 1907.

Legend in pencil: *Coping on office building Hall. Owatonna Bank. March 27/07.* Dimensions in pencil except *2'0"* and *K* which are in red pencil.
Pencil.
4 3/16 x 7 7/8 in.   10.6 x 20.0 cm.
Drawn by George Elmslie.

119. CEILING ORNAMENT,   (Fig. 52)   FLLW/LHS No. 79
dated May 21, 1907.

Legend lettered in pencil: *Owatonna Bank ceiling ornament. May 21/07. Scale
1 1/2" = 1 foot.* Notations in pencil, upper right: *run*, bottom: *Wall, run*, and
dimensions.
Pencil.
7 7/8 x 11 7/8 in.   20.0 x 30.0 cm.
Drawn by George Elmslie.

120. ORNAMENTAL CLOCK   (Fig. 53)   FLLW/LHS Nos. 77 and 119
FRAME, dated June 12, 1907.

Legend lettered in pencil: *Clock Frame. Owatonna Bank. Scale 1 1/2" = 1 foot.
L. H. Sullivan Archt. June 12/07.* Notations in pencil, left edge: *terra cotta band
around vault*, upper right: *Panel*, left side of clock: *Solid to this line, Perforated*,
clock face: *dial, 30" open*, lower left: *1 1/2" Roman Brick*, and dimensions.
Pencil.
11 7/8 x 7 13/16 in.   30.1 x 19.8 cm.
Drawn by George Elmslie.

121. ORNAMENTAL PIER,   (Fig. 50)   FLLW/LHS Nos. 117 and 118
1907.

Pencil.
6 3/8 x 9 1/8 in.   16.2 x 23.1 cm.
Drawn by George Elmslie.

Of the many drawings prepared for the highly ornate National Farmers' Bank at
Owatonna, Minnesota, only these six remain.[45] With the exception of No. 118, a study
sketch by Elmslie, all are scaled working drawings of various ornamental areas. In spite
of Elmslie's apparently greatly increased role in ornamenting the Owatonna Bank, it is
unlikely that, even here, Elmslie worked entirely without guidance. Although Elmslie is
said to have contributed one or two elements to the overall design,[46] the building is certainly Sullivan's own. Where the decorative details were to go and exactly how they were
to be visually integrated into the building was also surely decided by Sullivan. Presumably Sullivan also made small sketches of each ornament from which Elmslie later
worked when detailing the ornament. That Sullivan thus controlled the early stages of
design helps to account for the higher quality of the Owatonna ornaments and the better
integration of them into the total composition than was usual in Elmslie's independent
work.

Elmslie's drawing for the cornice, ceiling ornament, and clock frame (Nos. 117, 119,
and 120) were carried out exactly as designed and are still in place in the bank (Figs.

[45] Three of these were in two pieces when they
were acquired by the Avery Library and inadvert-
ently each part was given a separate number. Although the parts are now reunited, the result is that
three of the Owatonna drawings now carry two
FLLW/LHS numbers.

[46] For a more detailed discussion of the Owa-
tonna ornaments see Paul E. Sprague, "The National
Farmers' Bank, Owatonna, Minnesota," *Prairie
School Review*, IV (Second Quarter, 1967), 5-21.

51-53). His drawings of an ornamental panel (No. 116) and pier (No. 121) for the adjoining office building were executed but not exactly as designed (Fig. 50). Apparently Elmslie's sketch for a coping in the office building (No. 118) was never carried any further, and this may account for its preservation.

GIBSON'S MAGAZINE COVER

122. COVER DESIGN FOR *GIBSON'S*   FLLW/LHS No. 82
MAGAZINE, dated February 11, 1910.

> Inscribed in pencil: *LHS. Feb. 11–'10.* Lettered in pencil on the design, top to bottom: *Volume Two. Number Four. Gibson's Magazine. March 1910. Price Ten Cents.* Sullivan's monogram.
> Pencil.
> 8 1/2 x 4 1/16 in.   21.6 x 10.3 cm.

David Gibson, an editor and publisher of trade journals at Cleveland, Ohio, knew Sullivan through Gibson's brother Louis, who had been a classmate of Sullivan at the Massachusetts Institute of Technology.[47] Apparently Gibson prevailed on Sullivan in 1910 to design an artistic cover for a journal that he had founded several years earlier.[48] That Gibson did so is extremely fortunate, for without this drawing we would have very little idea of Sullivan's ornamental style between 1900 and 1920. Since Sullivan allowed his draftsmen considerable freedom during these years in working out the details of his architectural ornament, it is difficult to assess the evolution of Sullivan's style on the basis of executed ornament. Only three other ornamental drawings by Sullivan are preserved from these two decades: the first (No. 115), dated 1902, seems atypical and therefore unreliable as a guide to Sullivan's ornamental style after the turn of the century. The second and third, made in 1917 and 1918 respectively (Figs. 60, 62),[49] belong without question to Sullivan's last ornamental style.

What the Gibson drawing tells us, when it is compared to Sullivan's earlier and later ornamental work, is that by 1910 Sullivan had already evolved, though perhaps not perfected, his late style of ornament. While elements like the curving stalks in the Gibson drawing are probably derived from similar motifs of the 1890's, such as appear in Sullivan's cover of 1896 for *Music* (Fig. 48), it is the character of the Gibson stalks with leaves clustered at the ends of limpid drooping branches that makes the Gibson drawing so definitely a part of Sullivan's last style (Figs. 60-63). It is also the segregation of motifs in the Gibson drawing, as well as the relatively succulent character of its organic forms, that relates the drawing more closely to the drawings of Sullivan's last years than to the ones of the 1890's.

[47] Letter from David Gibson to Hugh Morrison, Feb. 4, 1936, in the Hugh Morrison files.

[48] Published in Cleveland between 1908 and 1916 according to the *Union List of Serials.*

[49] The one, owned by Wilbert Hasbrouck, is an ornamental drawing for the Peoples Saving & Loan Association Bank at Sidney, Ohio, dated October 3, 1917. The other, drawn by Sullivan for his friend George Nimmons on September 25, 1918, is now in the collection of the Chicago School of Architecture Foundation.

SELECTED BIBLIOGRAPHY

THEORETICAL WRITINGS BY SULLIVAN

"Ornament in Architecture," *Engineering Magazine*, III (August 1892), 633-44. Reprinted in *Kindergarten Chats and Other Writings*, New York, 1947, pp. 187-90.

"Emotional Architecture as Compared with Intellectual: A Study in Objective and Subjective," *Inland Architect*, XXIV (November 1894), 32-34. Reprinted in *Kindergarten Chats and Other Writings*, pp. 191-201.

"The Tall Office Building Artistically Considered," *Lippincotts' Magazine*, LVII (March, 1896), 403-9. Reprinted in *Kindergarten Chats and Other Writings*, pp. 202-13.

"Kindergarten Chats," *Interstate Architect*, II (February 16, 1901)–III (February 8, 1902). Reprinted as *Kindergarten Chats*, edited by Claude Bragdon, Lawrence, Kansas: Scarab Fraternity Press, 1934. [This is the best edition though difficult to find. When Sullivan revised these articles in 1918 he made changes which diluted and confused his original thesis.] Reprinted in *Kindergarten Chats* (revised 1918) *and Other Writings*, edited by Isabella Atley, New York: Wittenborn, Schultz, 1947, pp. 17-174.

Democracy: A Man-Search. Edited by Elaine Hedges. Detroit: Wayne State University Press, 1961. Written 1907-1908.

"The Autobiography of an Idea," *Journal of the American Institute of Architects*, X (June 1922)–XI (September 1923). Reprinted as *The Autobiography of an Idea*, New York, American Institute of Architects, 1924. Reprinted by Dover, 1956. [The reader is advised to study the Bragdon edition of *Kindergarten Chats* before turning to this late work, ostensibly straightforward but in reality filled with hidden meanings.]

A System of Architectural Ornament According with a Philosophy of Man's Powers, New York: American Institute of Architects, 1924, plates dated January 1922 - May 1923. In some places Sullivan's argument is incomprehensible because some of the explanations prepared to appear on the plates were omitted when the plates were printed. For these see the original drawings at the Burnham Library, The Art Institute of Chicago. Sullivan's essay in the *System* is a condensation of the themes developed in "Kindergarten Chats."

BOOKS AND THESES ON SULLIVAN

Morrison, Hugh S. *Louis Sullivan: Prophet of Modern Architecture*. New York: W. W. Norton, 1935. Reprinted 1962. Bibliography, photographs.

Wright, Frank Lloyd. *Genius and the Mobocracy*. New York: Duell, Sloan and Pearce, 1949. Reprinted by Horizon Press, 1971. Drawings, photographs.

Kaufmann, Edgar (ed.). *Louis Sullivan and the Architecture of Free Enterprise*. Chicago: The Art Institute of Chicago, 1956. Bibliography. Catalogue of the Sullivan Exhibition at The Art Institute, 1956.

Nickel, Richard. "A Photographic Documentation of the Architecture of Adler & Sullivan." M.A. Thesis, Illinois Institute of Technology, 1957. Photographs, building list, bibliography.

Connely, Willard. *Louis Sullivan as He Lived*. New York: Horizon Press, 1960. Bibliography.

Bush-Brown, Albert. *Louis Sullivan*. New York: George Braziller, 1960. Photographs.

Paul, Sherman. *Louis Sullivan: An Architect in American Thought*. Englewood Cliffs, N.J.: Prentice-Hall, 1962. Notes, Bibliography.

Sprague, Paul. "The Architectural Ornament of Louis Sullivan." Unpublished Ph.D. dissertation, Princeton University, 1968.

Slade, Thomas M. "A Collated Edition of Louis H. Sullivan's *Kindergarten Chats*." Unpublished M.A. Thesis, State University of New York at Buffalo, 1971.

Articles on Sullivan

Kimball, Fiske. "Louis Sullivan: an Old Master," *Architectural Record*, LVII (April 1925), 289-304.

Wright, Frank Lloyd. Review of *Louis Sullivan* by Hugh Morrison, *Saturday Review of Literature*, XIII (December 14, 1935), 6. Reprinted in the *Journal of the Society of Architectural Historians*, XX (October 1961), 141-42.

Morrison, Hugh. Letter, *Saturday Review of Literature*, XIII (February 8, 1936), 9.

Elmslie, George G. Letter to Frank Lloyd Wright, dated June 12, 1936, in *Journal of the Society of Architectural Historians*, XX (October 1961), 140-41.

Tallmadge, Thomas. "Louis H. Sullivan," *Dictionary of American Biography*. Edited by Dumas Malone. New York: Charles Scribner's Sons, 1936, XXVIII, 196-97.

Elmslie, George. "Sullivan Ornamentation," *Journal of the American Institute of Architects*, VI (October 1946), 155-58.

Hope, Henry R. "Louis Sullivan's Architectural Ornament," *Magazine of Art*, XL (March 1947), 111-17; *Architectural Review*, CII (October 1947), 111-14.

Morrison, Hugh S. Review of *Genius and the Mobocracy* by Frank Lloyd Wright, *Magazine of Art*, XLIV (April 1951), 154-55.

Manson, Grant "Sullivan and Wright, an Uneasy Union of Celts," *Architectural Review*, CXVIII (November 1955), 297-300.

Johnson, Philip. "Is Sullivan the Father of Functionalism?" *Art News*, LV (December 1956), 45-46.

Scully, Vincent. "Louis Sullivan's Architectural Ornament," *Perspecta, the Yale Architectural Journal*, V (1959), 73-80.

Gebhard, David. "Louis Sullivan and George Grant Elmslie," *Journal of the Society of Architectural Historians*, XIX (May 1960), 62-68.

Hedges, Elaine. Introduction to *Democracy: A Man Search*, by Louis H. Sullivan. Detroit: Wayne State University Press, 1961, pp. vii-xxiv.

Gebhard, David. Review of *Democracy: A Man Search*, by Louis Sullivan; *A System of Architectural Ornament*, by Louis Sullivan; and *Louis Sullivan*, by Albert Bush-Brown, *Journal of the Society of Architectural Historians*, XXI (December 1962), 194-95.

Sprague, Paul E. "Adler & Sullivan's Schiller Building," *Prairie School Review*, II (Second Quarter, 1965), 5-20.

Sprague, Paul E. "The National Farmers' Bank, Owatonna, Minnesota," *Prairie School Review*, IV (Second Quarter, 1967), 5-21.

Vaughn, Edward J. "Sullivan and the University of Michigan," *Prairie School Review*, VI (First Quarter, 1969), 21-23.

MAJOR COLLECTIONS

Lotos Club Notebook. Student notebook with entries and drawings by Louis Sullivan, John Edelmann and others dating 1872-1880. The Avery Library, Columbia University.

Drawings by Louis Sullivan, his brother Albert, and Sullivan's mother and father, dated 1849-1885. Burnham Library, The Art Institute of Chicago.

Drawings by Louis Sullivan, dated 1873-1910. The Frank Lloyd Wright Collection. The Avery Library, Columbia University.

Drawings by Louis Sullivan, dated 1875-1881. Emil Lorch papers, Michigan Historical Collections, Bentley Historical Library of the University of Michigan, Ann Arbor, Michigan.

Drawings by Louis Sullivan: three are full-size drawings of ornamental details of the Wainwright Tomb, St. Louis, 1892, and one is of a screen for Andrew O'Connor, 1922. The University of Michigan Museum of Art, transfer from the College of Architecture and Design.

Miscellaneous architectural drawings. Burnham Library, The Art Institute of Chicago.

Miscellaneous architectural drawings. The Avery Library, Columbia University.

Sketches and drawings for *A System of Architectural Ornament*, 1922-1923. Burnham Library, The Art Institute of Chicago.

INDEX

Vaughn, Edward T., 53

wainscot, 37
Wainwright Building, *see* St. Louis, Mo.
Wainwright Tomb, *see* St. Louis, Mo.
Western Architect, 11
Western Association of Architects, 54

Whitman, Walt, 54
Wineman House, *see* Chicago, Ill.
winged-figures, *see* Transportation Building
Wright, Frank Lloyd, 3, 9, 28, 31, 32, 37, 47;
    Drawings for a Living Architecture, 35;
    Genius and the Mobocracy, 7n, 13-14, 14n,
    19, 25, 29, 35-36, 45

Library of Congress Cataloging in Publication Data

Sullivan, Louis H   , 1856-1924.
    The drawings of Louis Henry Sullivan.

    Bibliography: p.
    Includes index.
    1. Sullivan, Louis H., 1856-1924—Catalogs.
2. Wright, Frank Lloyd, 1869-1959—Art collections—
Catalogs.   3. Columbia University. Libraries.
Avery Architectural Library—Catalogs.   I. Sprague,
Paul E.   II. Columbia University. Libraries. Avery
Architectural Library.   III. Title.
NA2707.S94A4 1978   720'.22'2   78-51192
ISBN 0-691-03924-0

CATALOGUE DRAWINGS

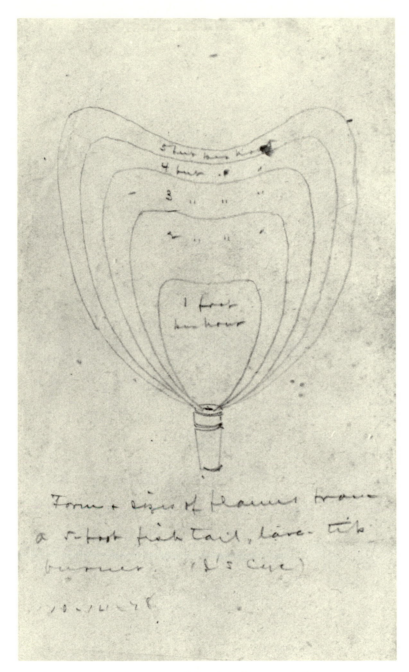

No. 1. Study of a Flame. Pencil. Louis Sullivan. c. 1872.

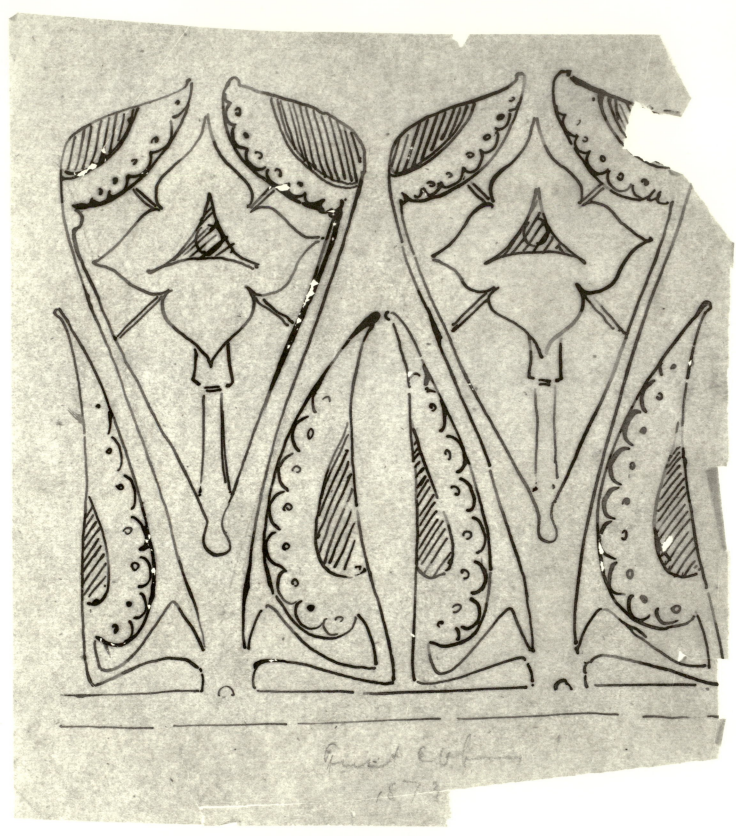

No. 2. Fresco Design [?]. Purple ink on tracing paper. Louis Sullivan. 1873.

No. 3. Fresco Design [?]. Purple ink on tracing paper. Louis Sullivan. 1873.

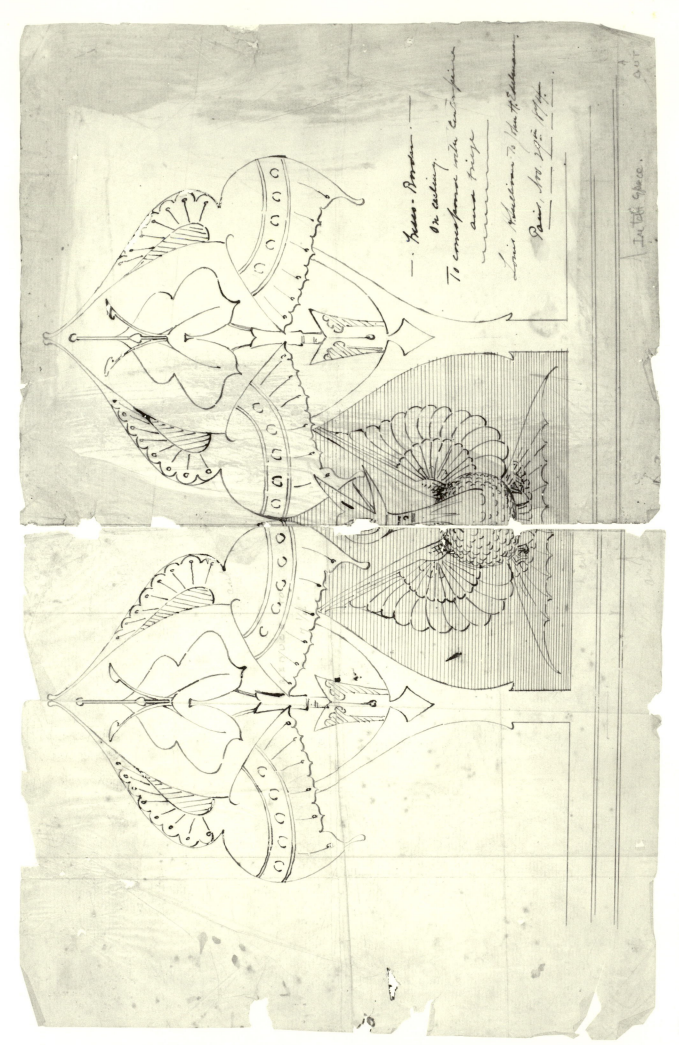

No. 4. Fresco Design. Purple ink on tracing paper. Louis Sullivan. November 29, 1874.

No. 5. Fresco Design. Ink on tracing paper. Louis Sullivan. April 1, 1875.

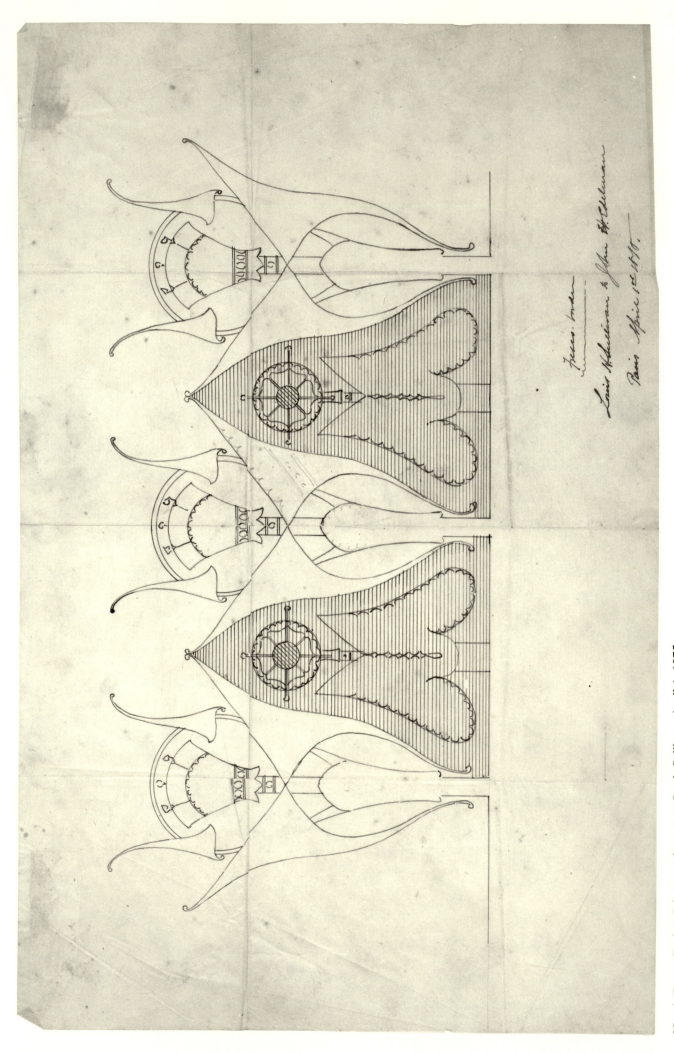

No. 6. Fresco Design. Ink on tracing paper. Louis Sullivan. April 1, 1875.

Center-piece in fresco.

Louis H Sullivan, July 11th 1875

No. 7. Fresco Design. Ink on tracing paper. Louis Sullivan. July 11, 1875.

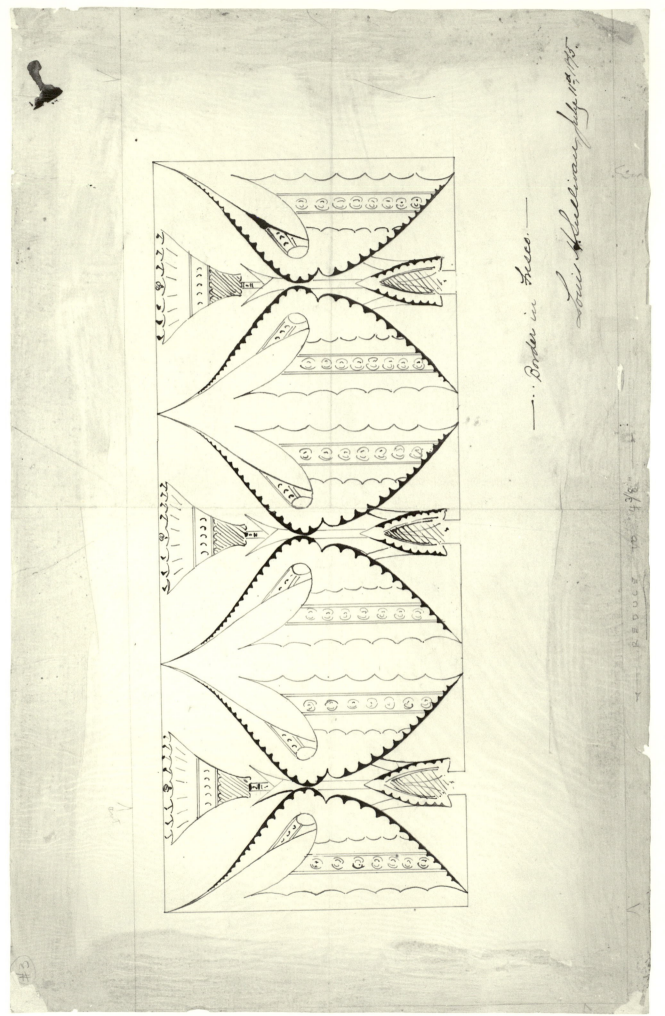

— Border in Fresco. —

Louis H Sullivan July 11th 1875.

No. 8. Fresco Design. Ink on tracing paper. Louis Sullivan. July 11, 1875.

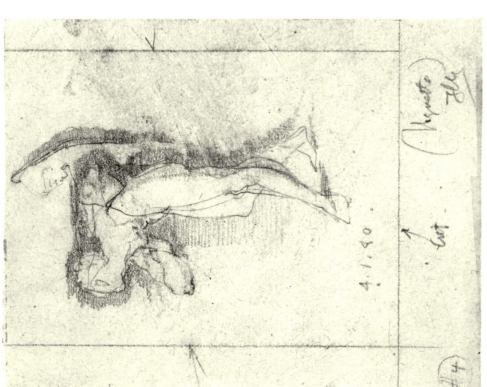

No. 9. A Nude Figure. Pencil on medium weight drawing paper.
Louis Sullivan. April 1, 1880.

No. 10. A Nude Figure. Pencil on medium weight drawing paper. Louis Sullivan. May 30, 1880.

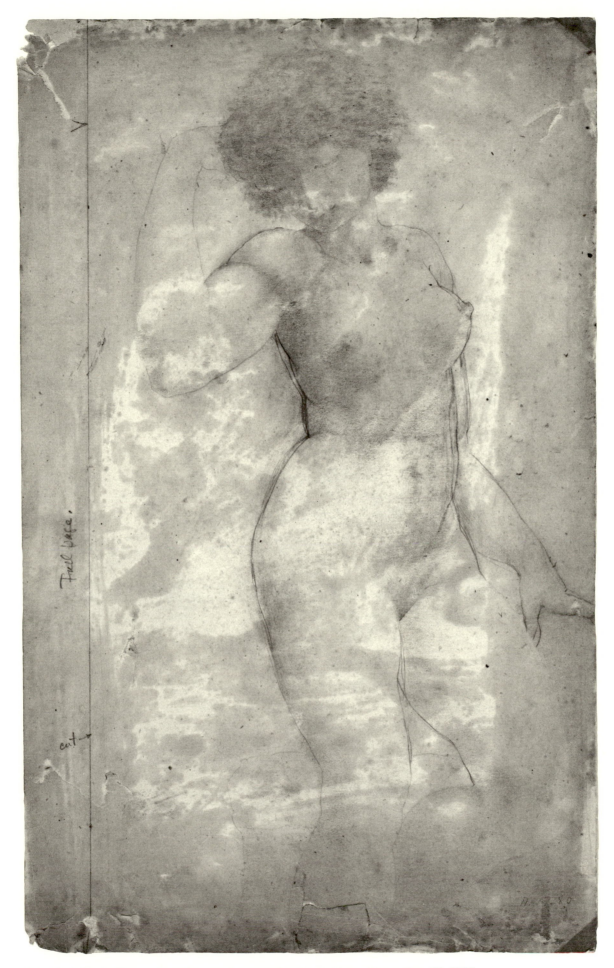

No. 11. A Nude Figure. Pencil on tracing paper. Louis Sullivan. November 17, 1880.

No. 12. Column Capital, Wineman House, Chicago,
Ill. Pencil on heavy drawing paper.
Louis Sullivan. c. July, 1882.

No. 13. Interior Wall with Boxes, McVicker's
Theater Remodeling, Chicago, Ill.
Pencil on drawing paper.
Louis Sullivan. January 9, 1883.

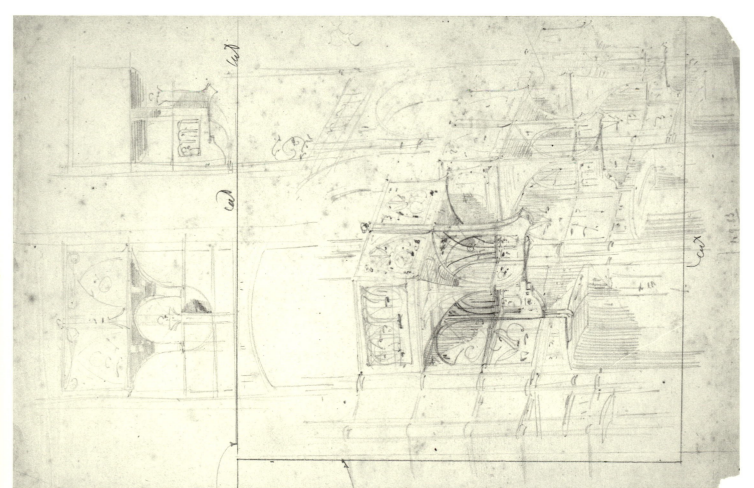

No. 14. Ornamental Design. Pencil. Louis Sullivan. May 6, 1884.

No. 15. Ornamental Study. Pencil on paper torn from a pad. Louis Sullivan. April 13, 1885.

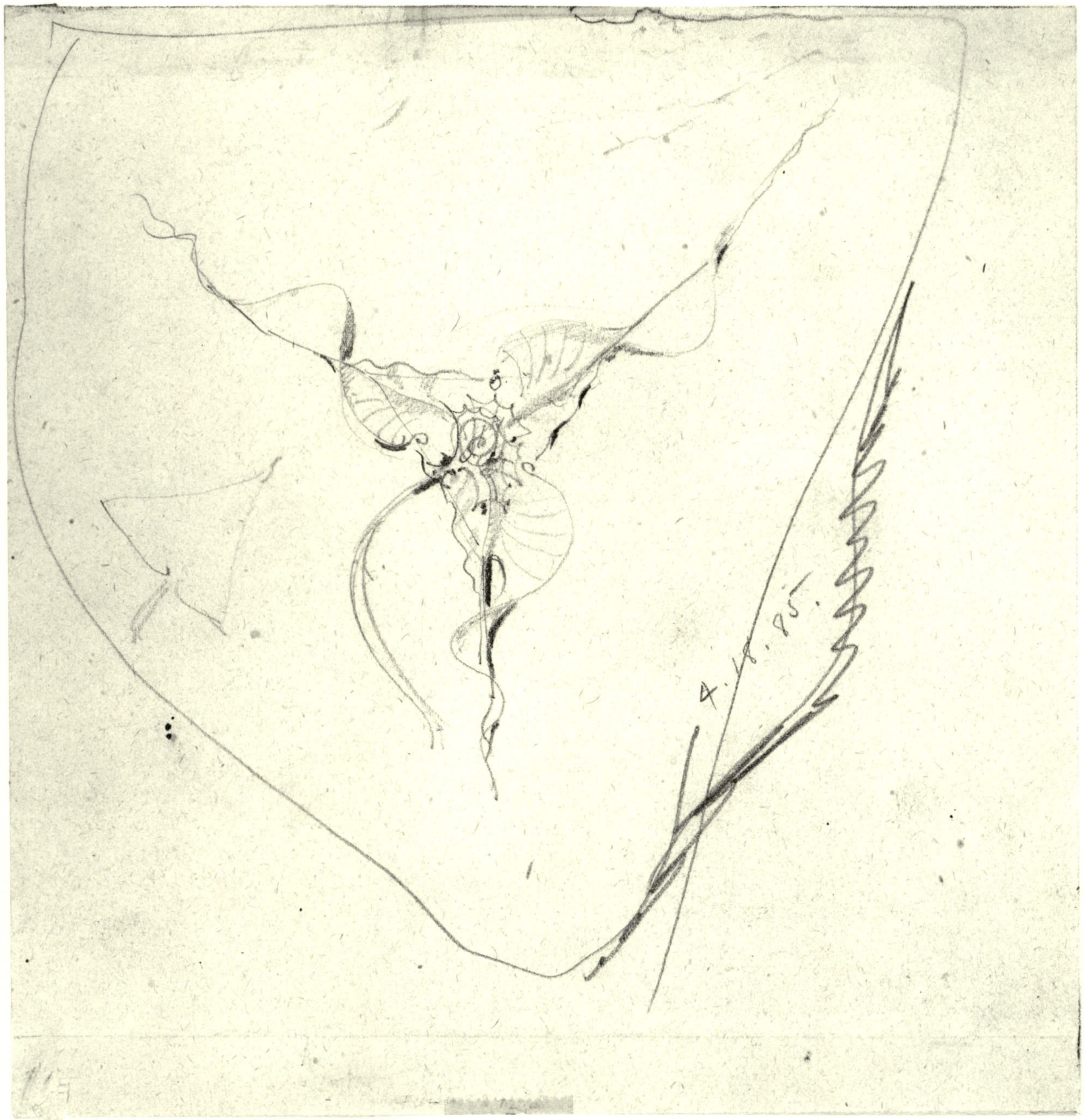

No. 16. Ornamental Study. Pencil.
Louis Sullivan. April 18, 1885.

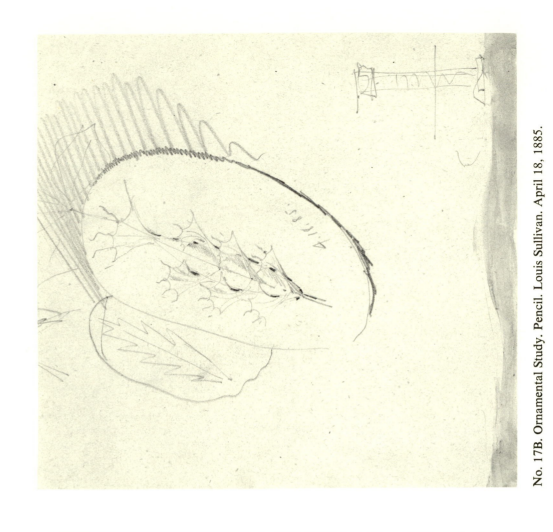

No. 17B. Ornamental Study. Pencil. Louis Sullivan. April 18, 1885.

No. 17A. Ornamental Study. Pencil. Louis Sullivan. April 18, 1885.

18

20

No. 18. Ornamental Study. Pencil
on paper torn from a pad.
Louis Sullivan.
April 18, 1885.

No. 20. Ornamental Study. Pencil
on paper torn from a pad.
Louis Sullivan.
August 23, 1885.

No. 19. Ornamental Study. Pencil on paper torn from a pad. Louis Sullivan. May 17, 1885.

No. 21. Ornamental Study. Pencil. Louis Sullivan.
August 23, 1885.

No. 22. Ornamental Study. Pencil. Louis Sullivan.
August 28, 1885.

No. 23. Ornamental Study. Pencil on paper torn from a pad. Louis Sullivan. December 18, 1885.

No. 24. Ornamental Design. Pencil. Louis Sullivan. September 30, 1885.

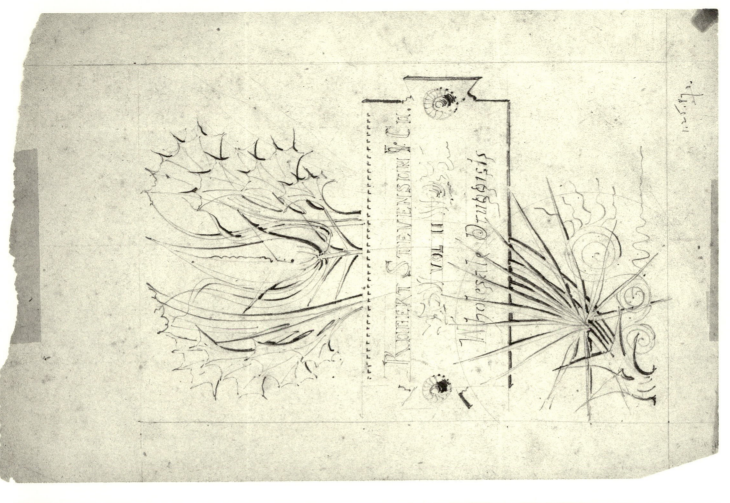

No. 25B. Cover Design, Wholesale Druggists' Catalogue. Pencil.
Louis Sullivan. January 25, 1887.

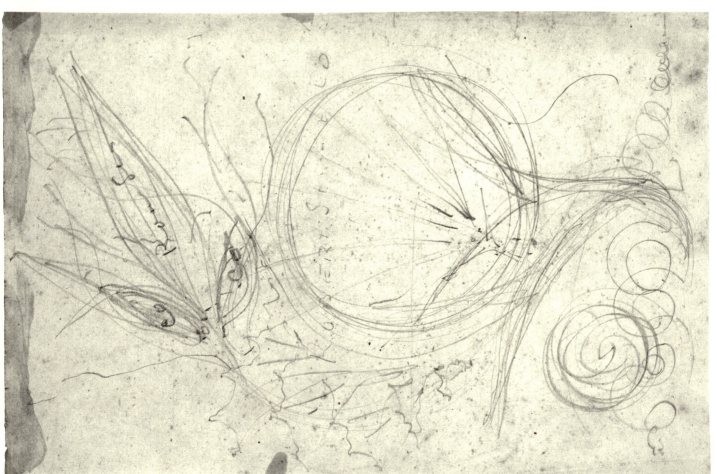

No. 25A. Cover Design, Wholesale Druggists' Catalogue. Pencil on
paper torn from a pad. Louis Sullivan. c. 1887.

No. 26. Ornamental Corbel, Auditorium Building, Chicago, Ill. Pencil on heavy-weight drawing paper. Louis Sullivan. July 23, 1888.

No. 27. Ornamental Corbel, Auditorium Building, Chicago,
Ill. Pencil. Louis Sullivan. 1888-1889.

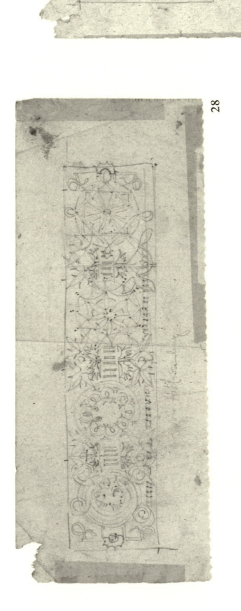

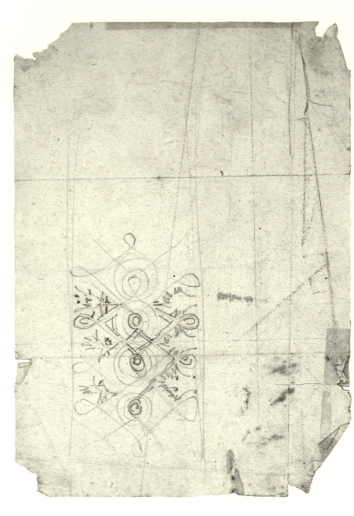

No. 28. Mosaic Stair Landing, Auditorium Building, Chicago, Ill.
Pencil on paper torn from a pad. Louis Sullivan. 1888-1889.

No. 29. Mosaic Stair Landing, Auditorium Building, Chicago, Ill.
Pencil on paper torn from a pad. Louis Sullivan. 1888-1889.

No. 30A. Mosaic Wall Decoration, Auditorium Building, Chicago, Ill.
Pencil. Louis Sullivan. 1888-1889.

No. 30B. Mosaic Decoration [?], Auditorium Building, Chicago, Ill.
Pencil. Louis Sullivan, 1888-1889.

No. 31. Newel Post, Auditorium Building, Chicago, Ill. Pencil on tracing paper.
Not drawn by Louis Sullivan. 1888-1889.

No. 32. Ornamental Capital, Auditorium Banquet Hall, Chicago, Ill. Pencil.
Louis Sullivan. April 15, 1890.

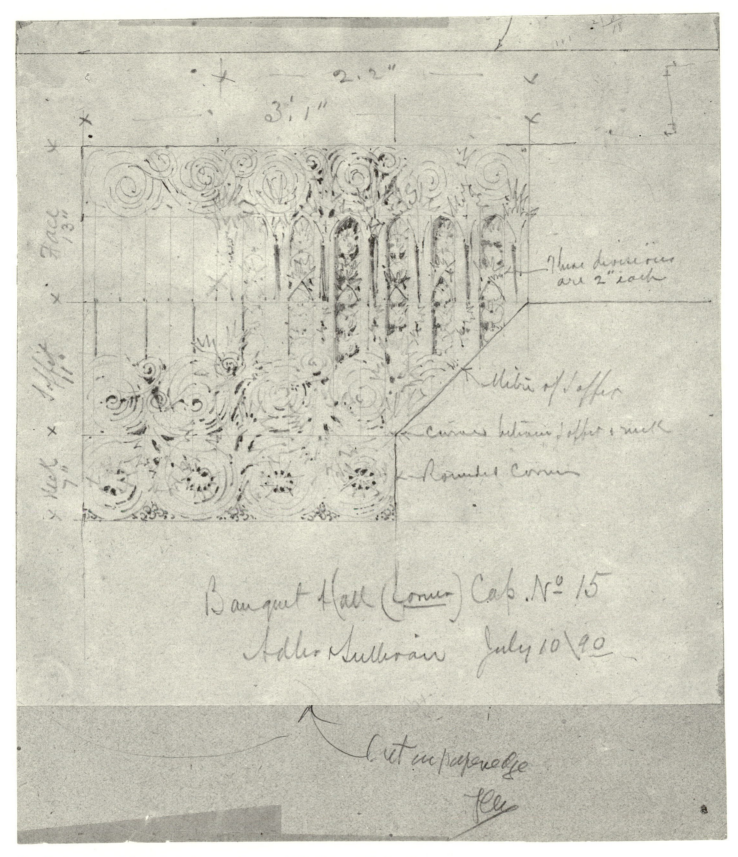

No. 33. Ornamental Capital, Auditorium Banquet Hall, Chicago, Ill. Pencil.
Louis Sullivan. July 10, 1890.

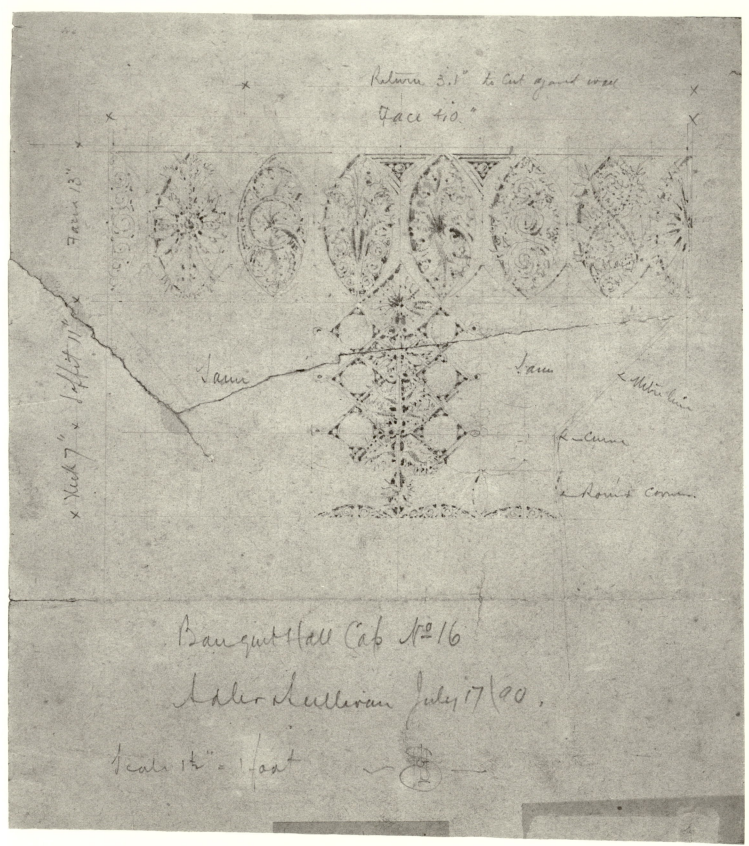

No. 34. Ornamental Capital, Auditorium Banquet Hall, Chicago, Ill. Pencil.
Louis Sullivan. July 17, 1890.

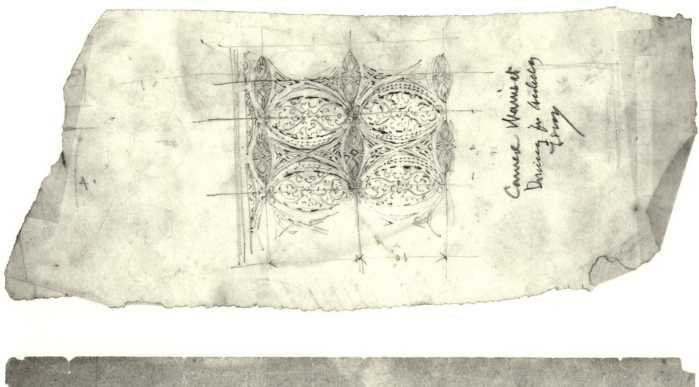

No. 36. Ornamental Design. Pencil on tracing paper. Not drawn by Sullivan. c. 1890.

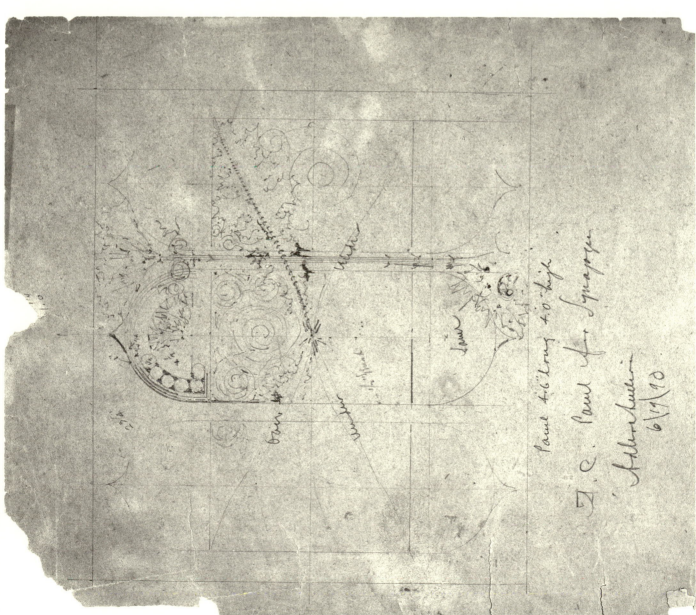

No. 35. Ornamental Panel. K.A.M. Synagogue, Chicago, Ill. Pencil. Louis Sullivan. June 19, 1890.

No. 37. Design for an Ornamental Frame. Pencil on tracing paper. Louis Sullivan. c. 1890.

No. 37 (detail)

No. 38. Ornamental Cornice, Getty Tomb, Chicago, Ill. Pencil on the back of a sheet of Adler & Sullivan stationery (left side) attached to a piece of plain paper (right side). Louis Sullivan. October 16, 1890.

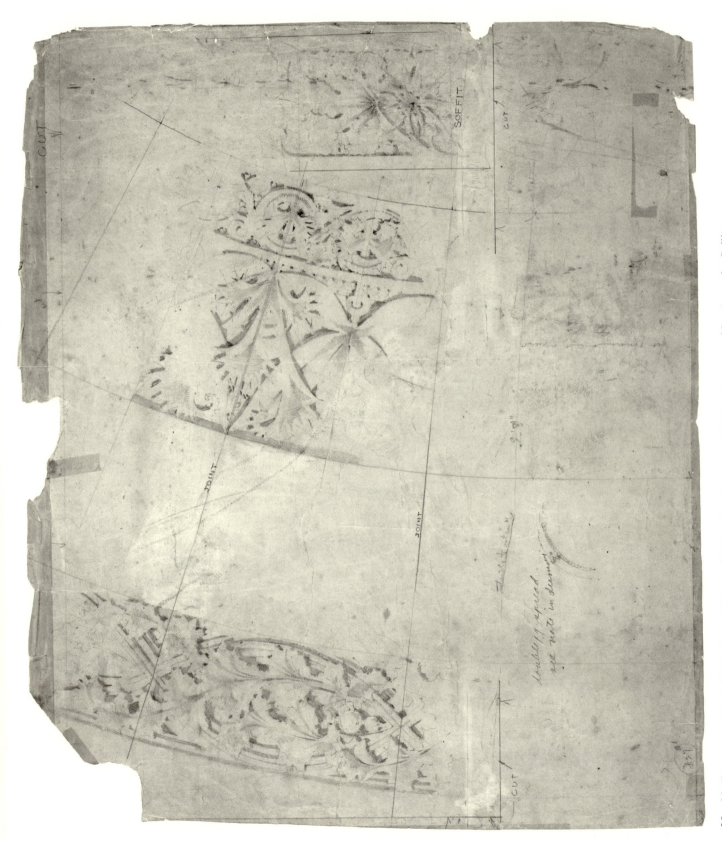

No. 39. Ornamental Arch, Getty Tomb, Chicago, Ill. Pencil on heavy-weight drawing paper. Not drawn by Sullivan.
c. October, 1890.

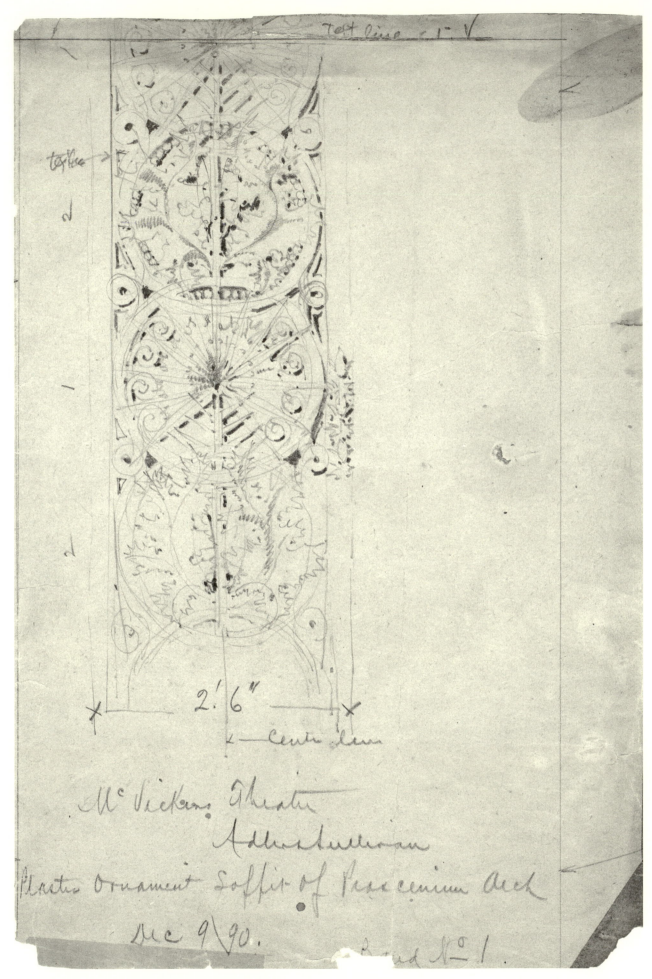

No. 40. Ornamental Soffit, McVicker's Theater Remodeling, Chicago, Ill. Pencil.
Louis Sullivan. December 9, 1890.

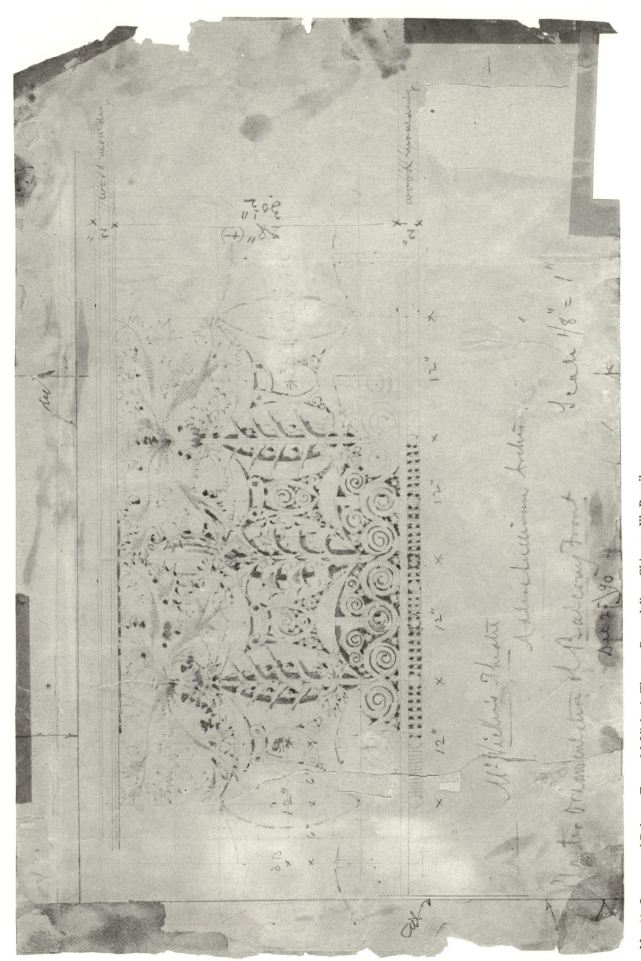

No. 41. Ornamental Balcony Front, McVicker's Theater Remodeling, Chicago, Ill. Pencil.
Louis Sullivan. December 25, 1890.

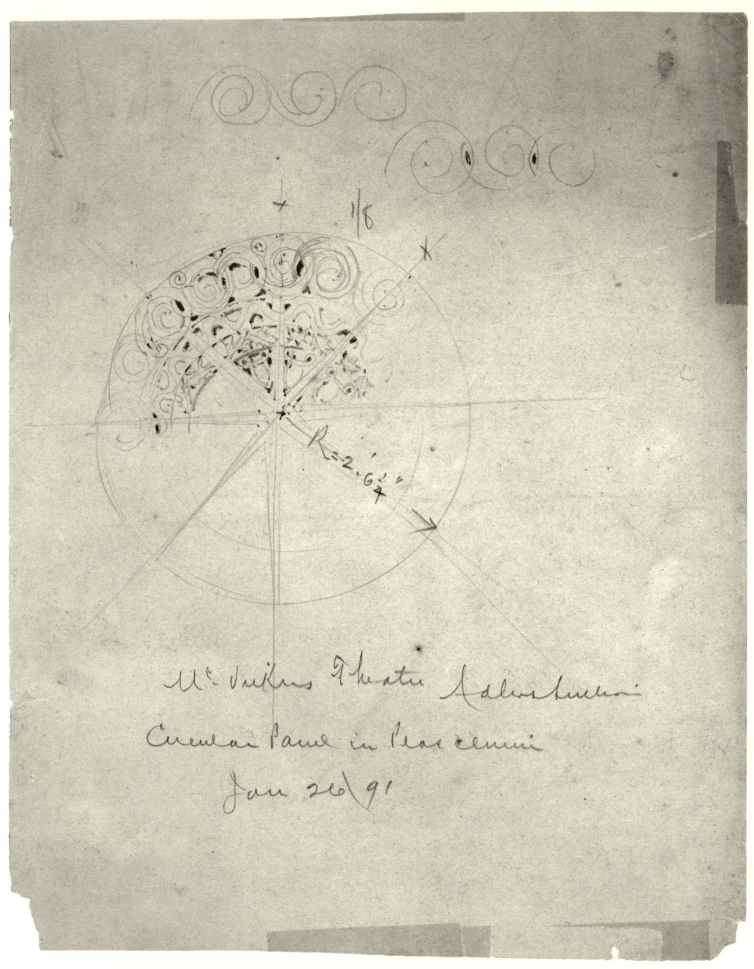

No. 42. Ornamental Panel, McVicker's Theater Remodeling, Chicago, Ill. Pencil.
Louis Sullivan. January 26, 1891.

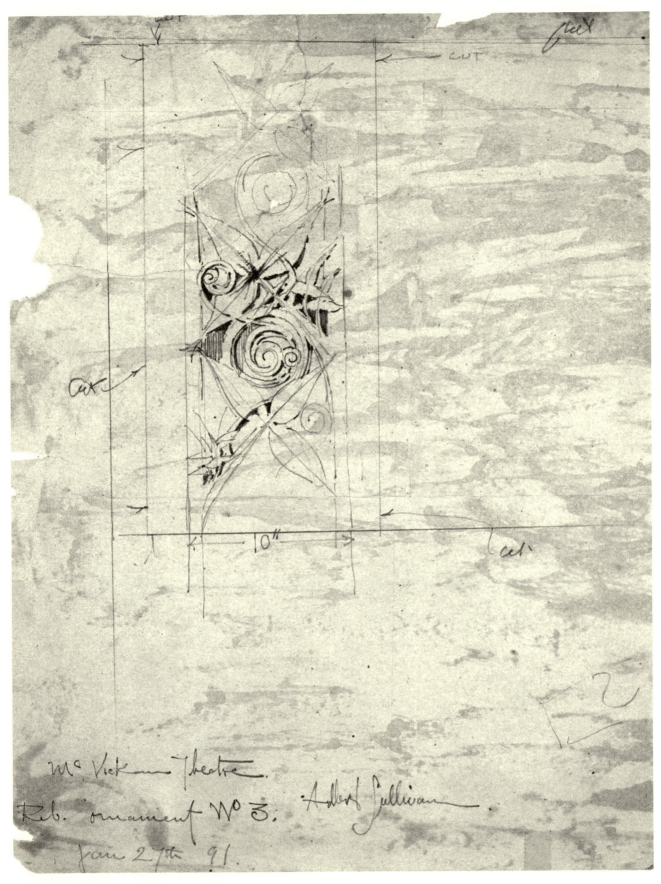

No. 43. Ornamental Rib, McVicker's Theater Remodeling, Chicago, Ill. Pencil.
Not drawn by Sullivan. January 27, 1891.

No. 44. Ornamental Band, McVicker's Theater Remodeling, Chicago, Ill. Pencil.
Louis Sullivan. February 2, 1891.

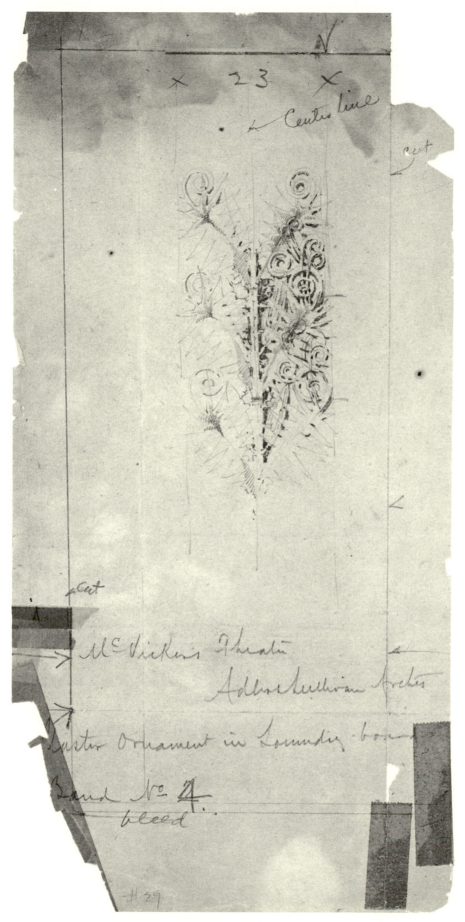

No. 45. Ornamental Band, McVicker's Theater Remodeling,
Chicago, Ill. Pencil. Louis Sullivan. 1890-1891.

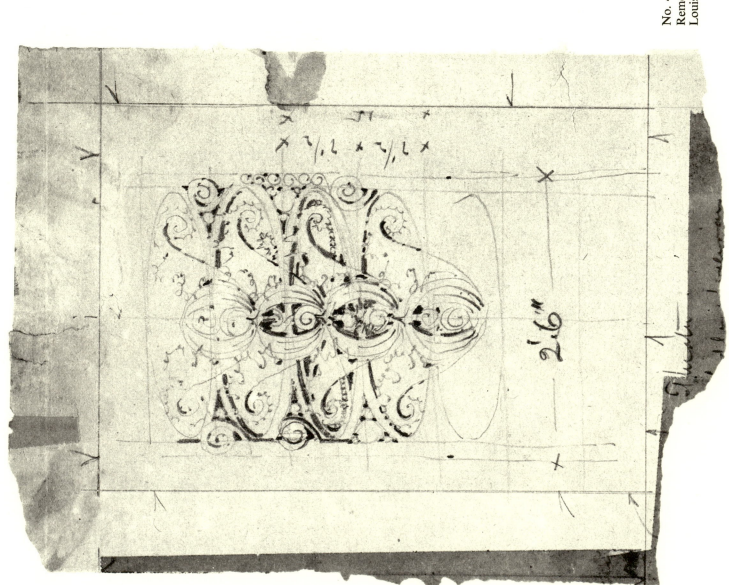

No. 46. Ornamental Band, McVicker's Theater Remodeling, Chicago, Ill. Pencil. Louis Sullivan. 1890-1891.

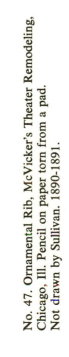

47

48

No. 47. Ornamental Rib, McVicker's Theater Remodeling,
Chicago, Ill. Pencil on paper torn from a pad.
Not drawn by Sullivan. 1890-1891.

No. 48. Ornamental Frieze, McVicker's Theater Remodeling,
Chicago, Ill. Pencil on paper torn from a pad.
Not drawn by Sullivan. 1890-1891.

No. 49. Ornamental Rib [?], McVicker's Theater Remodeling [?],
Chicago, Ill. Pencil. Not drawn by Sullivan. 1890-1891.

No. 50. Ornamental Rib [?], McVicker's Theater Remodeling [?],
Chicago, Ill. Pencil. Not drawn by Sullivan. 1890-1891.

No. 52. Ornamental Door Jamb, Transportation Building, Chicago, Ill.
Pencil. Louis Sullivan. September 23, 1891.

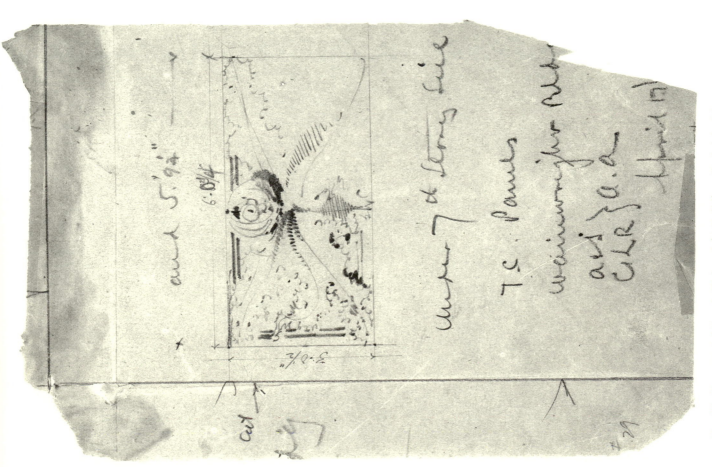

No. 51. Ornamental Panel, Wainwright Building, St. Louis, Mo.
Pencil. Louis Sullivan. April 17, 1891.

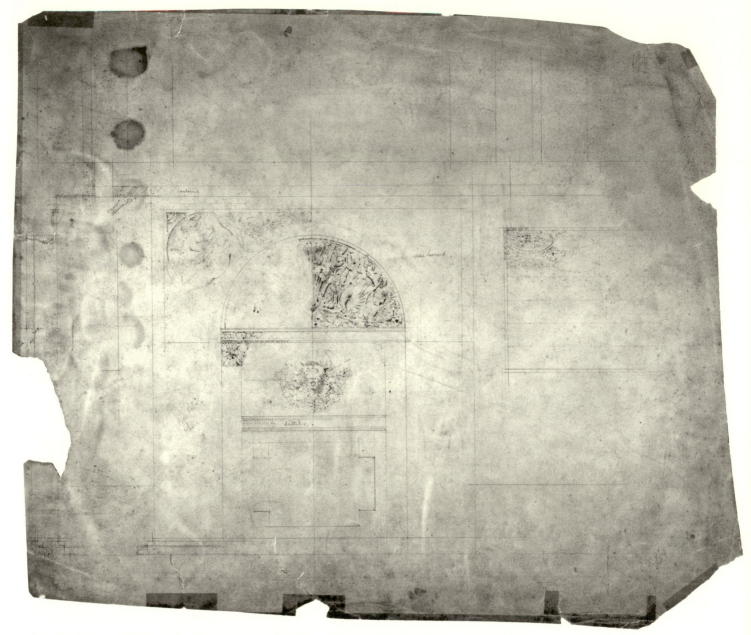

No. 53. Ornamental Fountain, Transportation Building, Chicago, Ill. Pencil on heavy-weight drawing paper. Louis Sullivan. 1891.

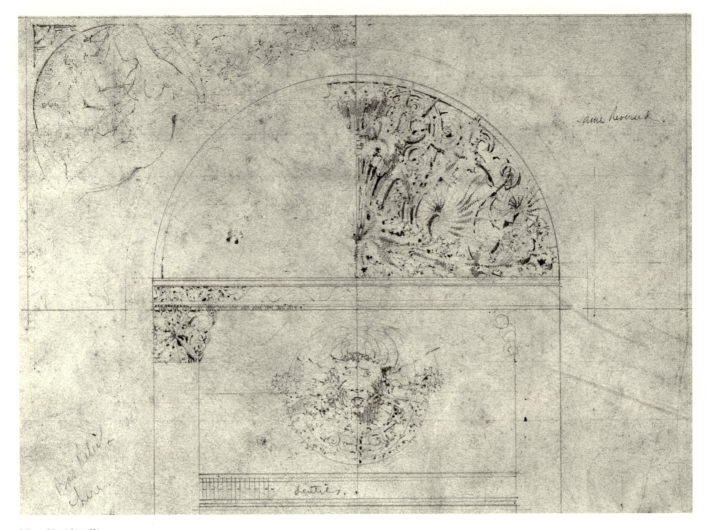

No. 53 (detail)

No. 54. Ornamental Fresco,
Transportation Building, Chicago, Ill.
Pencil on tracing paper. Tracing
not by Sullivan. 1891-1892.

No. 55. Ornamental Doorframe, Wainwright Tomb, St. Louis, Mo.
Pencil. Louis Sullivan. 1892.

No. 56. Ornamental Gate, Wainwright Tomb, St. Louis, Mo. Ink on linen.
Tracing by Frank Lloyd Wright. 1892.

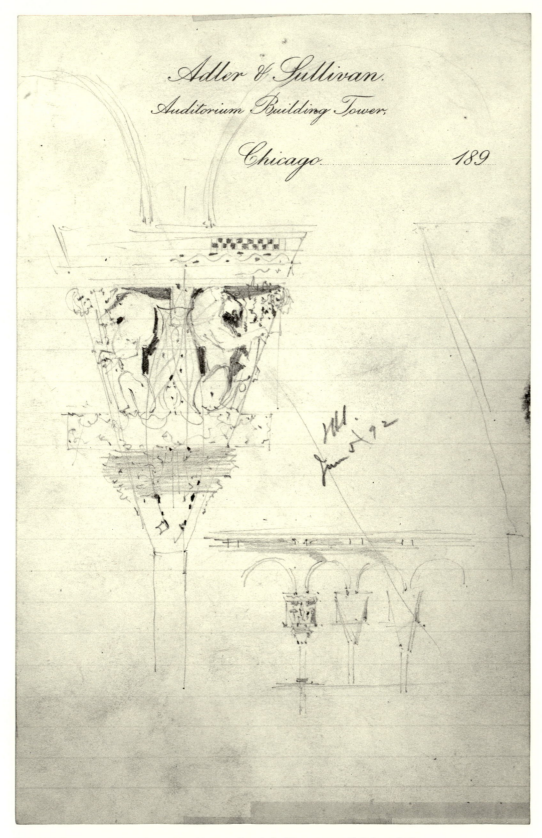

Adler & Sullivan.
Auditorium Building Tower.
Chicago 189

No. 57. Ornamental Gallery. Pencil on Adler & Sullivan paper lightly ruled.
Louis Sullivan. June 5, 1892.

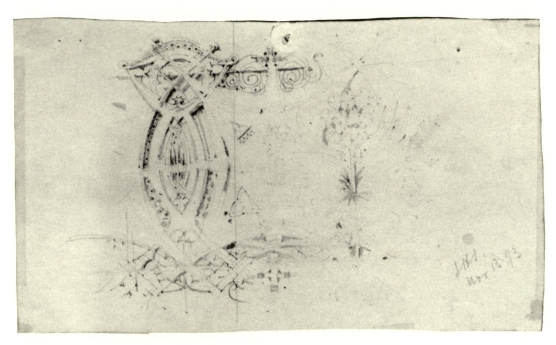

No. 58. Ornamental Design. Pencil. Louis Sullivan. November 13, 1893.

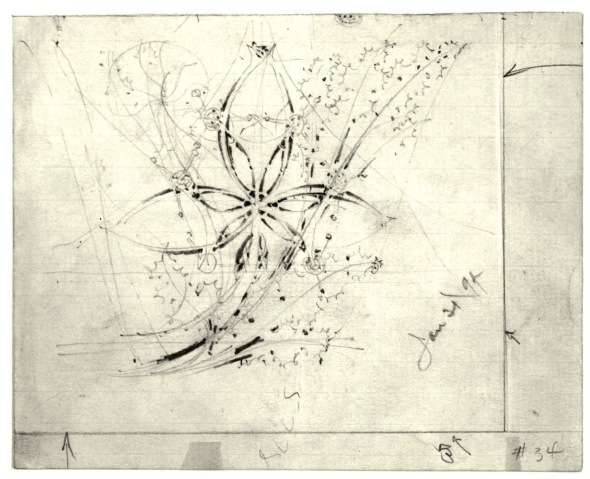

No. 59. Ornamental Study. Pencil. Louis Sullivan. January 31, 1894.

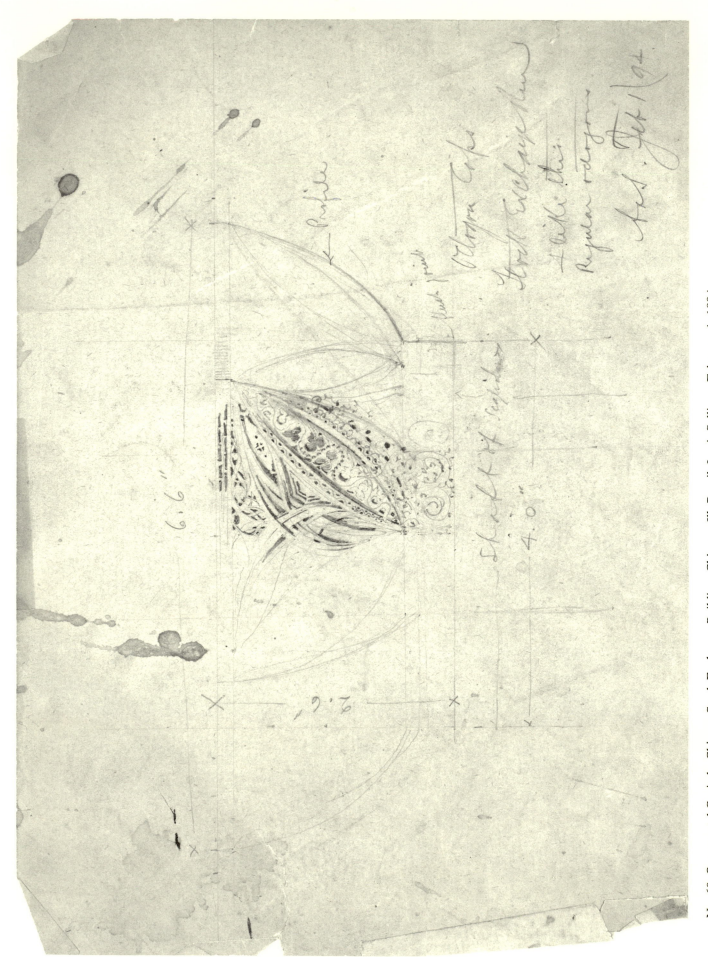

No. 60. Ornamental Capitals. Chicago Stock Exchange Building, Chicago, Ill. Pencil. Louis Sullivan. February 1, 1894.

No. 61. Ornamental Angle Block. Chicago Stock Exchange Building, Chicago, Ill. Pencil on heavy-weight drawing paper. Louis Sullivan. March 14, 1894.

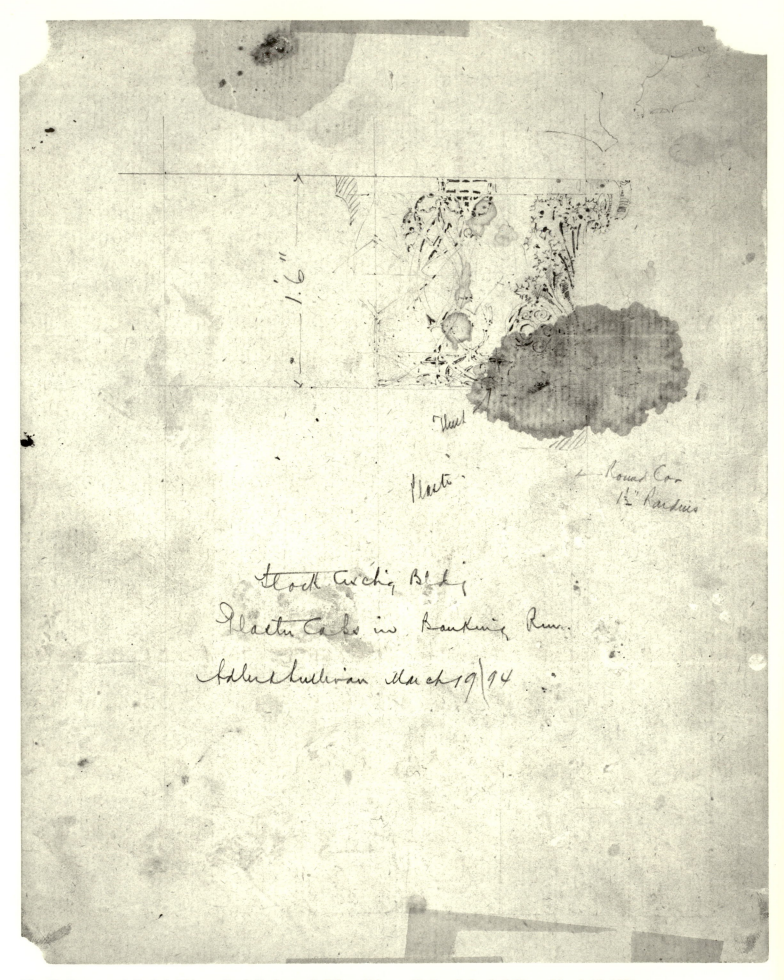

No. 62. Ornamental Capital, Chicago Stock Exchange Building, Chicago, Ill. Pencil. Louis Sullivan. March 19, 1894.

No. 64. Ornamental Capital, St. Nicholas Hotel, St. Louis, Mo. Pencil on
Adler & Sullivan stationery. Louis Sullivan. March 10, 1894.

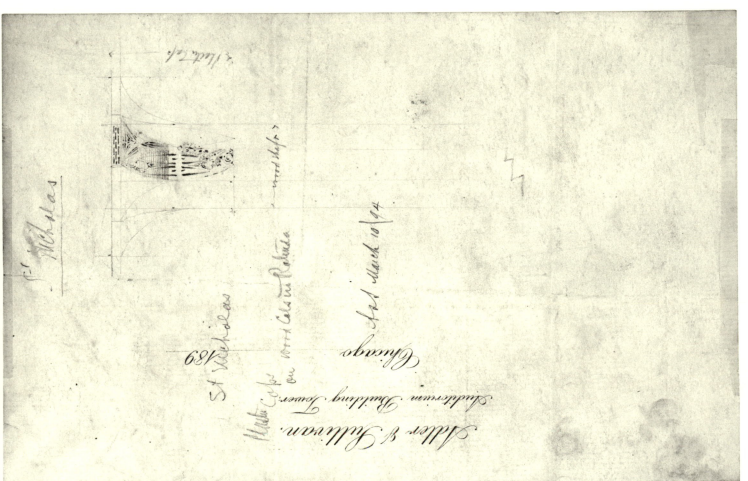

No. 63. Ornamental Capital, St. Nicholas Hotel, St. Louis, Mo. Pencil on
Adler & Sullivan stationery. Louis Sullivan. March 10, 1894.

No. 65. Ornamental Fireplace, St. Nicholas Hotel, St. Louis, Mo. Pencil on heavy-weight drawing paper. Louis Sullivan. May, 1894.

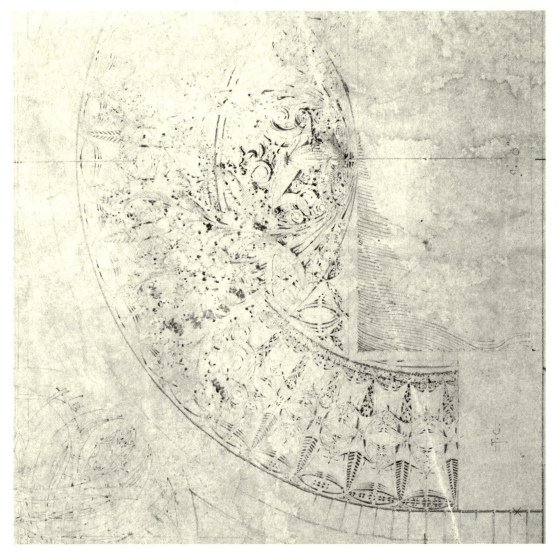

No. 65 (detail)

No. 65 (detail)

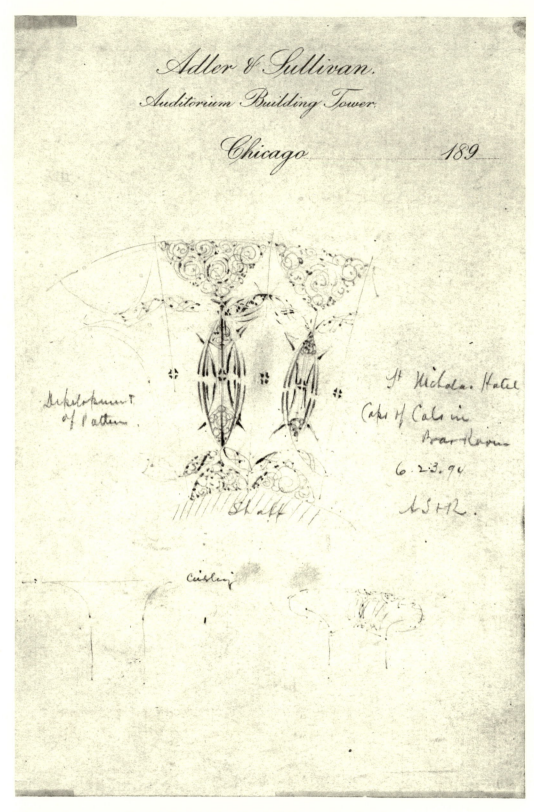

No. 66. Ornamental Capital, St. Nicholas Hotel, St. Louis, Mo. Pencil on
Adler & Sullivan stationery. Louis Sullivan. June 23, 1894.

No. 67. Ornamental Stencils, St. Nicholas Hotel, St. Louis, Mo. Pencil. Louis Sullivan. July 27, 1894.

(Drawn full size)

St Nicholas Hotel

July 28 94   A.L.H.

68

(Drawn full size)

St Nicholas

12" Color border thin dot

A.L.H. July 28 94

69

No. 68. Ornamental Stencil, St. Nicholas Hotel, St. Louis, Mo.
Pencil. Louis Sullivan. July 28, 1894.

No. 69. Ornamental Stencil, St. Nicholas Hotel, St. Louis, Mo.
Pencil. Louis Sullivan. July 28, 1894.

No. 70. Ornamental Stencil, St. Nicholas Hotel, St. Louis, Mo.
Pencil. Louis Sullivan. July 28, 1894.

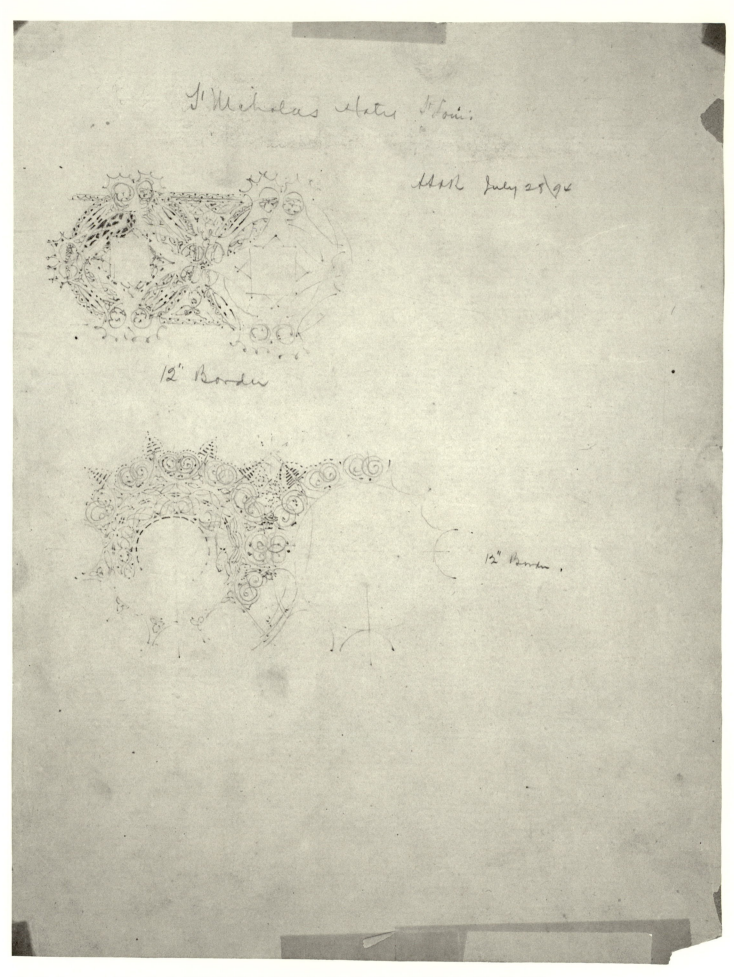

No. 71. Ornamental Stencils, St. Nicholas Hotel, St. Louis, Mo. Pencil. Louis Sullivan. July 28, 1894.

No. 72. Ornamental Stencil, St. Nicholas Hotel, St. Louis, Mo. Pencil. Louis Sullivan. July 31, 1894.

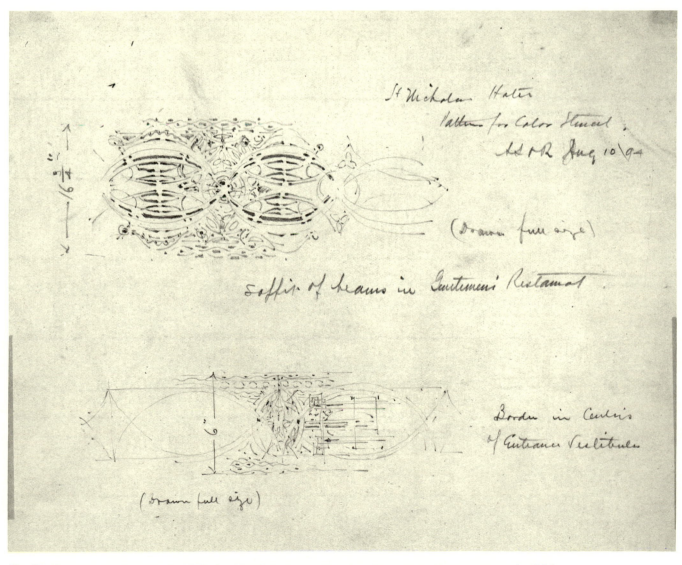

No. 73. Ornamental Stencils, St. Nicholas Hotel, St. Louis, Mo. Pencil. Louis Sullivan. August 10, 1894.

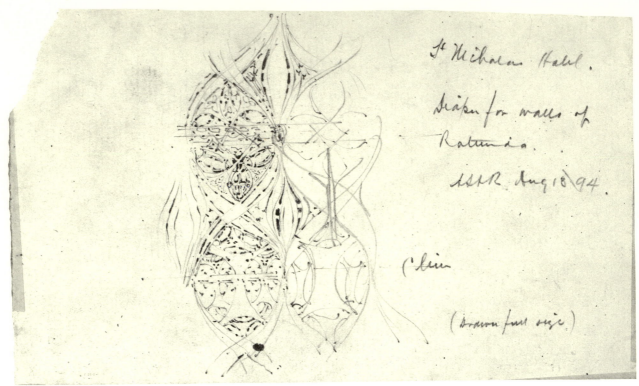

No. 74. Ornamental Stencils, St. Nicholas Hotel, St. Louis, Mo. Pencil.
Louis Sullivan. August 18, 1894.

No. 75. Ornamental Stencil, St. Nicholas Hotel, St. Louis, Mo. Pencil.
Louis Sullivan. September 20, 1894.

No. 76. Ornamental Stencils, St. Nicholas Hotel, St. Louis, Mo. Pencil.
Louis Sullivan. 1894.

St Nicholas Hall

12" Border in Ceiling
(sometimes Restaurant)

Sept 20. 94

75

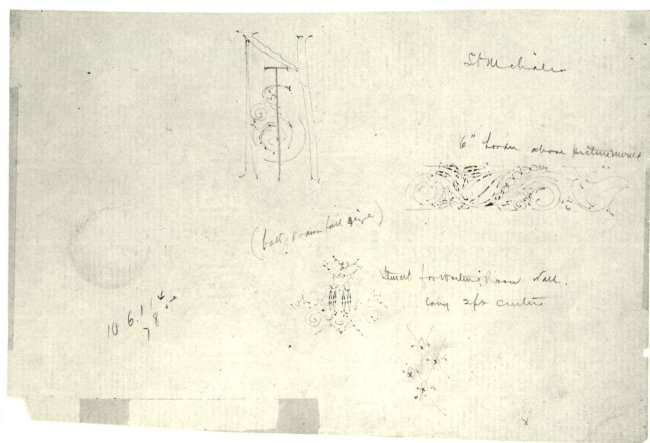

St Michaels

6" border above picture moulds

(half drawn full size)

Stencil for working Room wall
copy 2ft centers

10 6. 11 4
7 8"

76

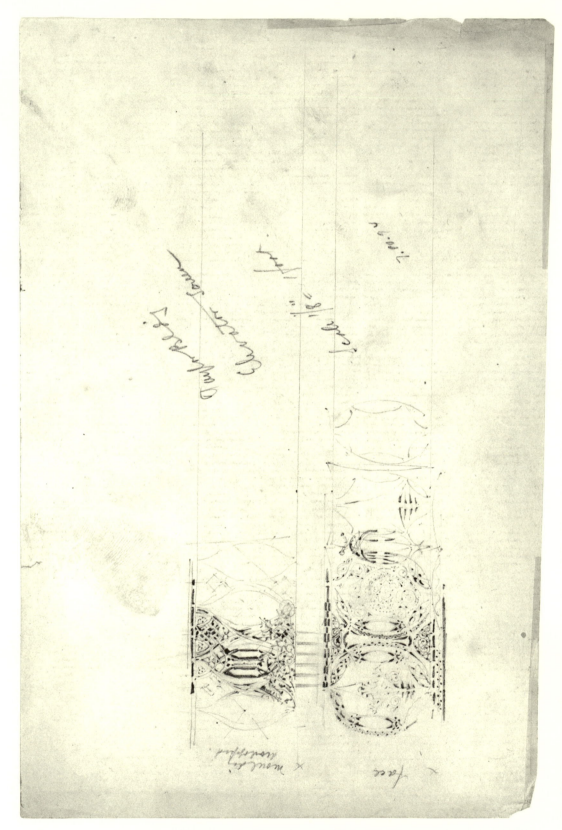

No. 77. Ornamental Elevator Screen, Taylor Building Remodeling, Chicago, Ill. Pencil.
Louis Sullivan. July 10, 1894.

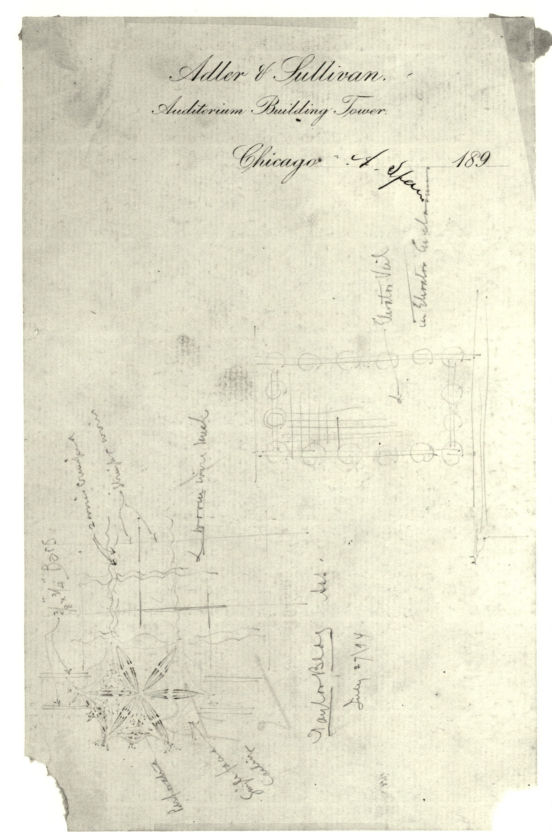

Adler & Sullivan.

Auditorium Building Tower.

Chicago _____ *189*

No. 78. Ornamental Elevator Screen, Taylor Building Remodeling, Chicago, Ill. Pencil on Adler & Sullivan stationery. Louis Sullivan. July 27, 1894.

Adler & Sullivan.

Auditorium Building Tower.

Chicago 189

79

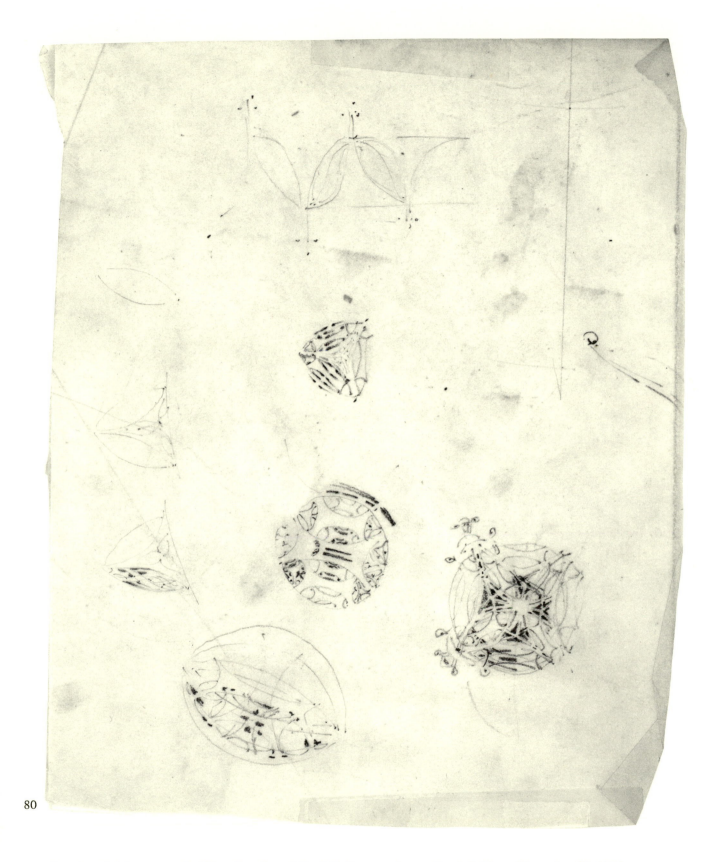

80

No. 79. Eliel Apartment Building. Pencil on Adler & Sullivan stationery. Louis Sullivan. November 28, 1894

No. 80. Ornamental Designs. Pencil on tracing paper. Louis Sullivan. c. 1894.

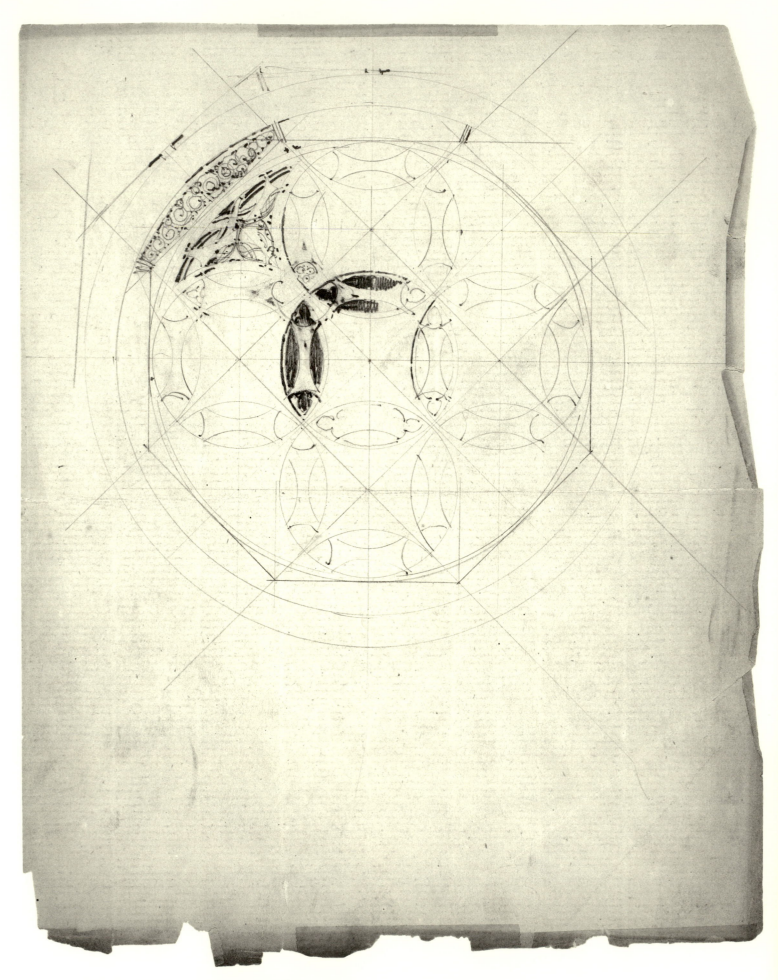

No. 81. Ornamental Design. Pencil. Louis Sullivan. c. 1894.

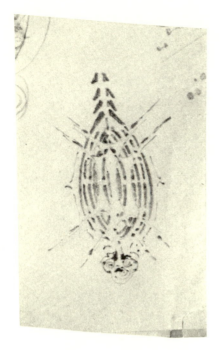

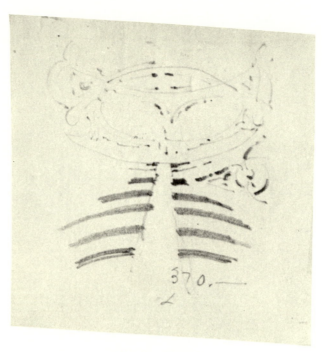

No. 82. Ornamental Design. Pencil.
Louis Sullivan. c. 1894.

No. 84. Ornamental Design. Pencil.
Louis Sullivan. c. 1894.

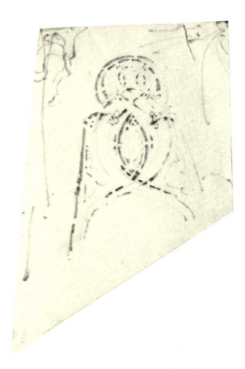

No. 85. Ornamental Design. Pencil.
Louis Sullivan. c. 1894.

No. 83. Ornamental Design. Pencil.
Louis Sullivan. c. 1894.

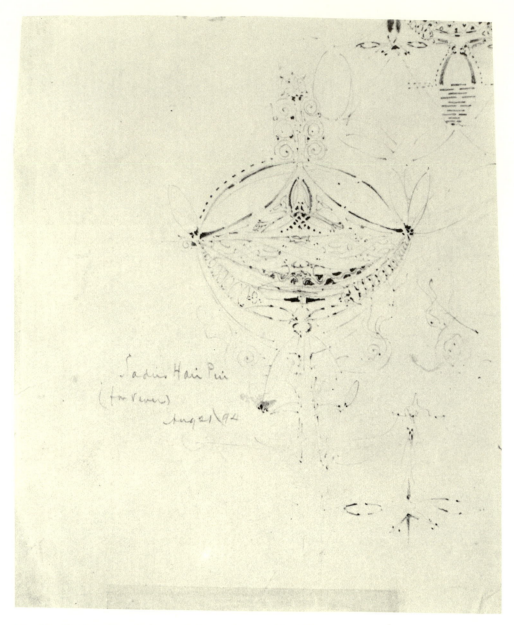

No. 86. Hairpin. Pencil. Louis Sullivan. August 21, 1894.

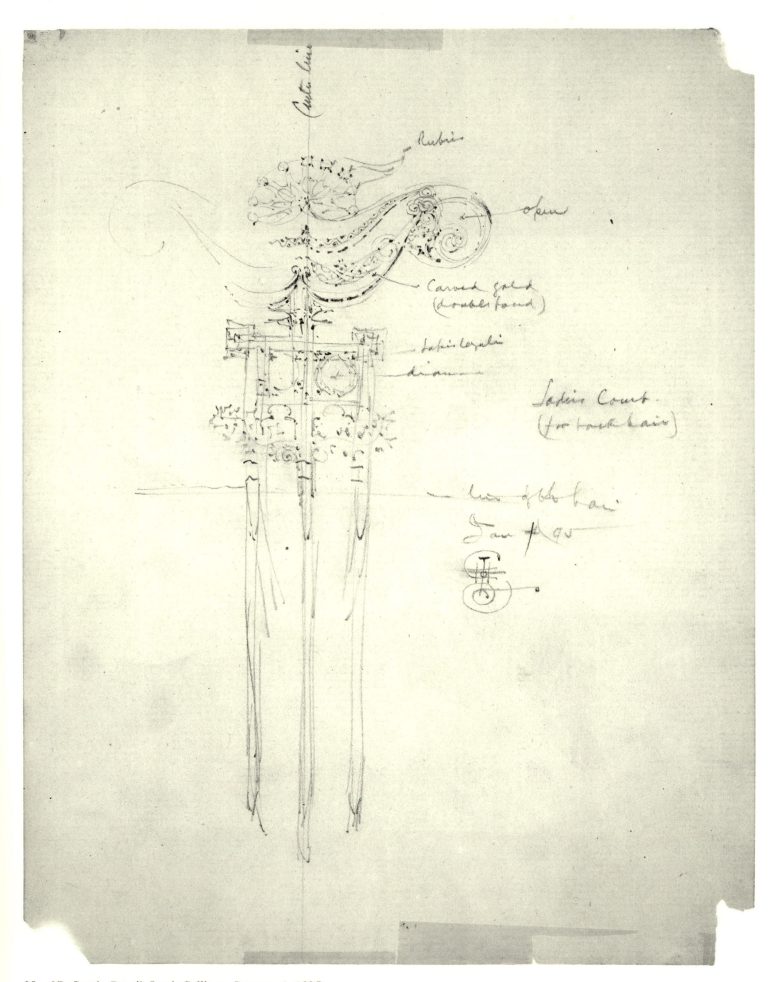

No. 87. Comb. Pencil. Louis Sullivan. January 4, 1895.

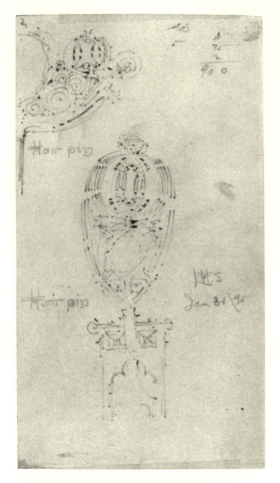

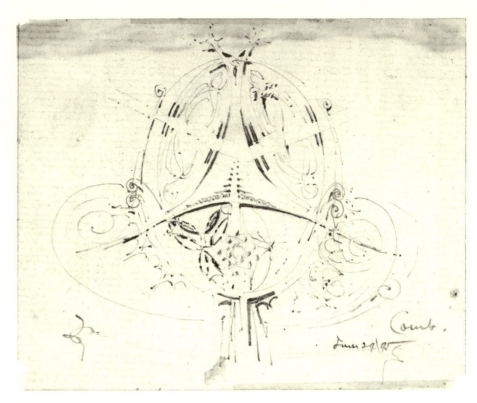

No. 88. Hairpins. Pencil. Louis Sullivan.
January 31, 1895.

No. 89. Comb. Pencil. Louis Sullivan.
June 29, 1895.

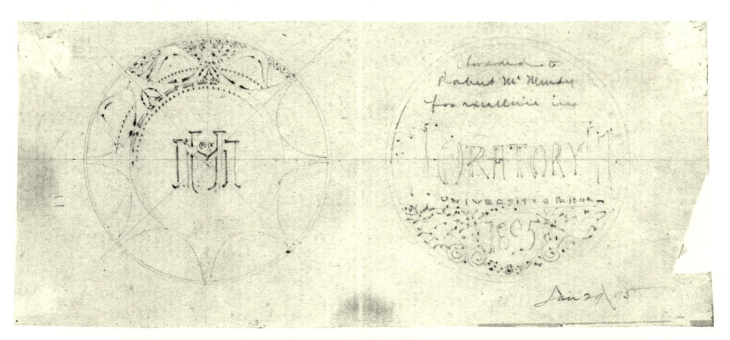

No. 90. Design for Oratory Medal. Pencil. Louis Sullivan. January 29, 1895.

Actual size 2½" diam.

H.S
Jan 30/95

No. 91. Design for Oratory Medal. Pencil. Louis Sullivan. January 30, 1895.

No. 92. Title Page Design. Pencil on medium-weight drawing paper. Louis Sullivan. March 5, 1895.

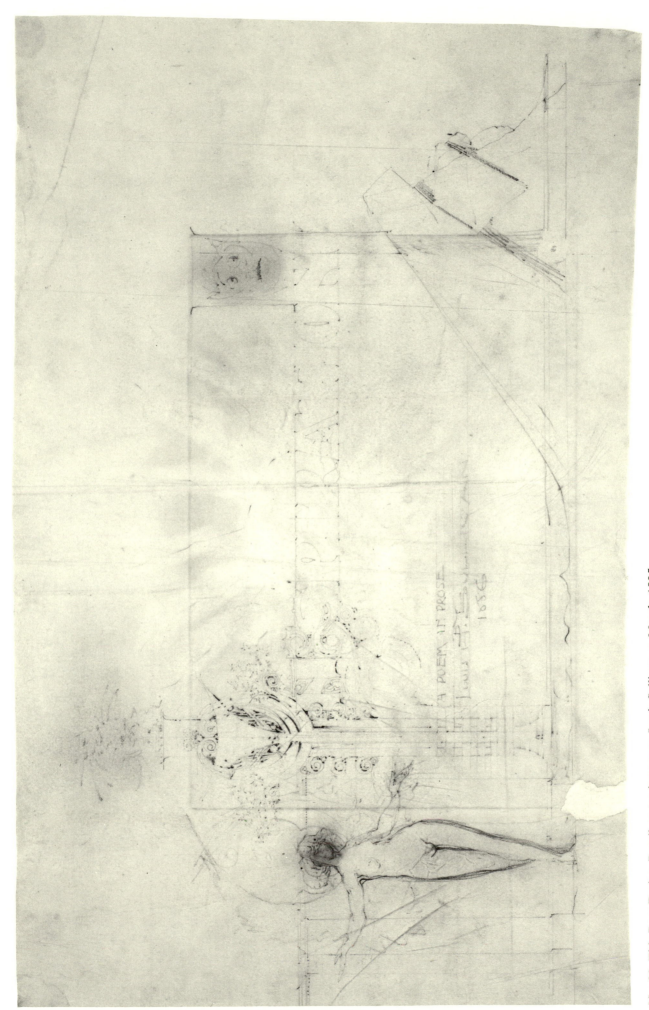

No. 93. Title Page Design. Pencil on tracing paper. Louis Sullivan. c. March, 1895.

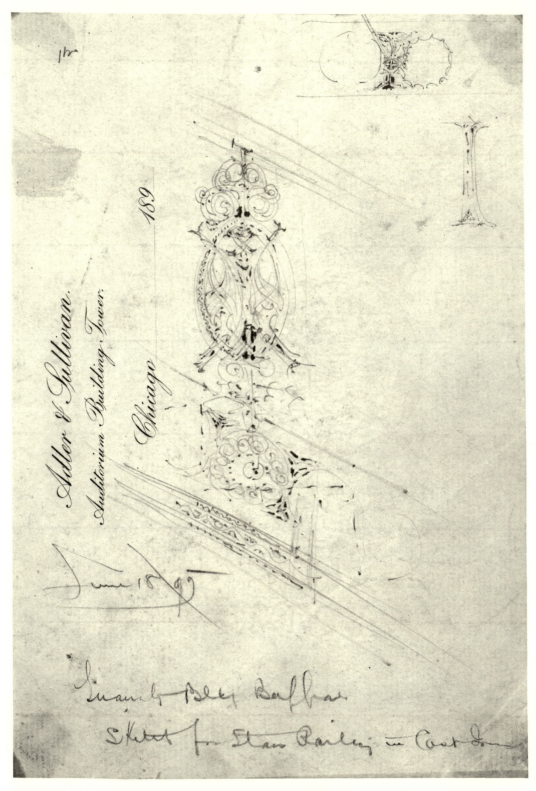

No. 94. Ornamental Stair Railing, Guaranty Building, Buffalo, N.Y. Pencil on
Adler & Sullivan stationery. Louis Sullivan. June 18, 1895.

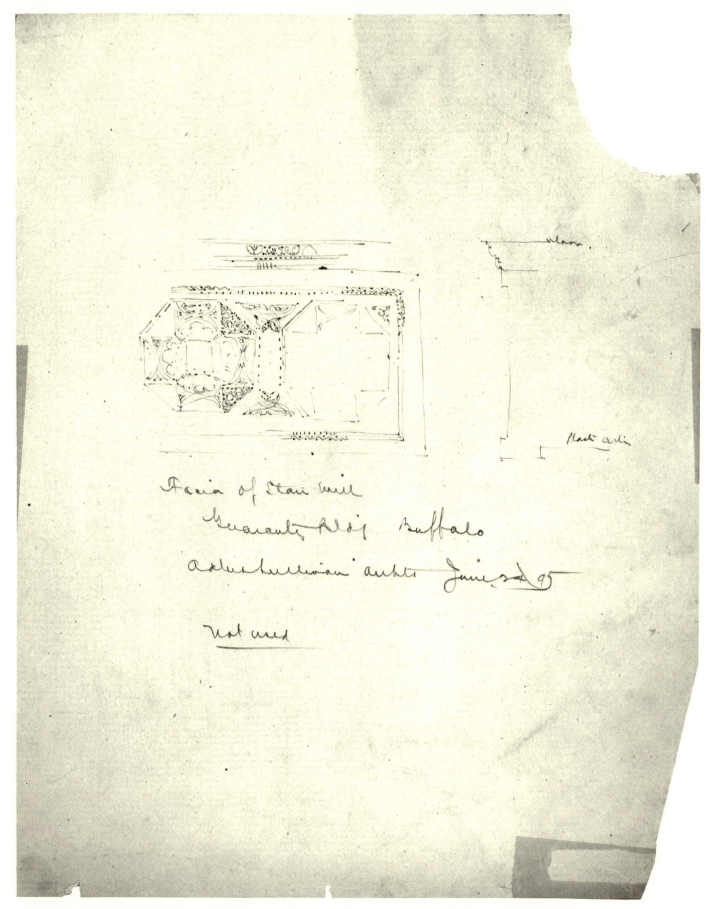

No. 95. Ornamental Fascia, Guaranty Building, Buffalo, New York. Pencil. Louis Sullivan. June 24, 1895.

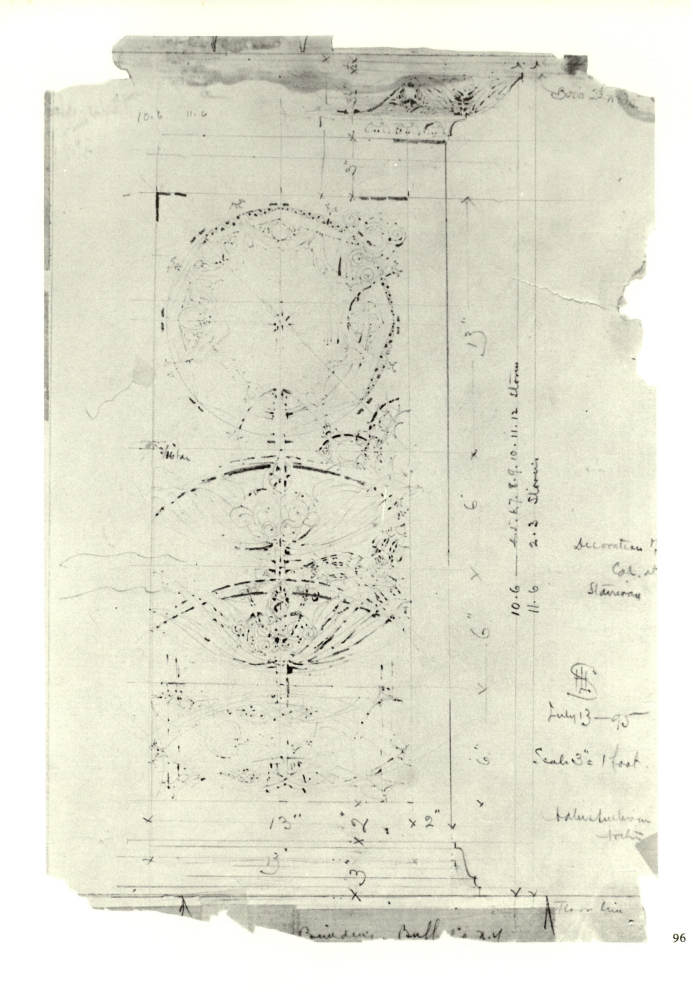

No. 96. Ornamental Pier, Guaranty Building, Buffalo, N.Y. Pencil. Louis Sullivan. July 13, 1895.

No. 97. Ornamental Doorplate, Guaranty Building, Buffalo, N.Y. Pencil. Louis Sullivan. July 18, 1895.

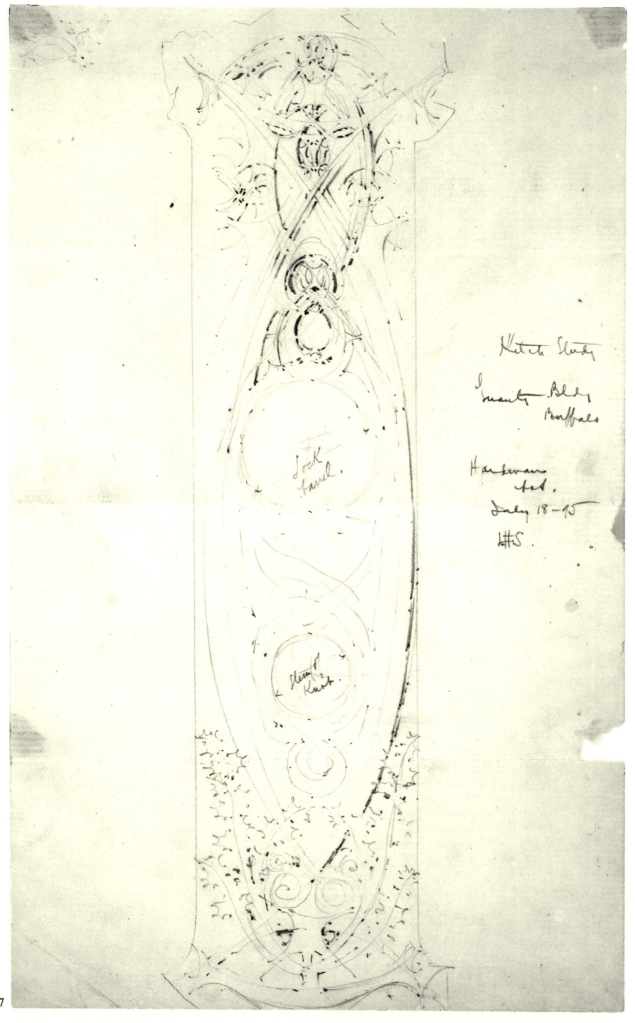

Sketch Study

Guaranty Bldg
Buffalo

Hardware
Set.
July 18 - 95

L#S.

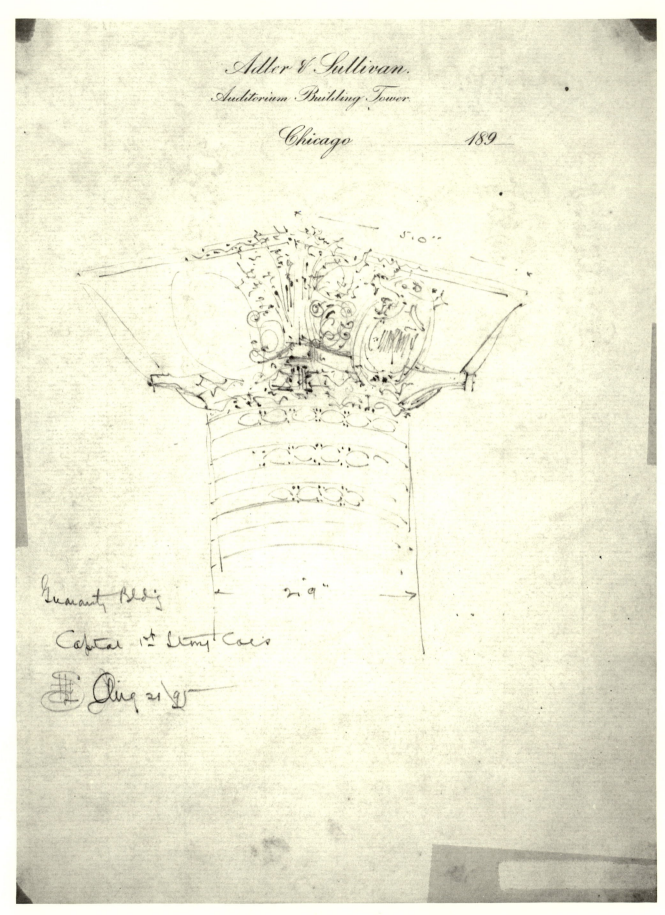

No. 98. Ornamental Capital, Guaranty Building, Buffalo, N.Y. Pencil on Adler & Sullivan stationery.
Louis Sullivan. August 21, 1895.

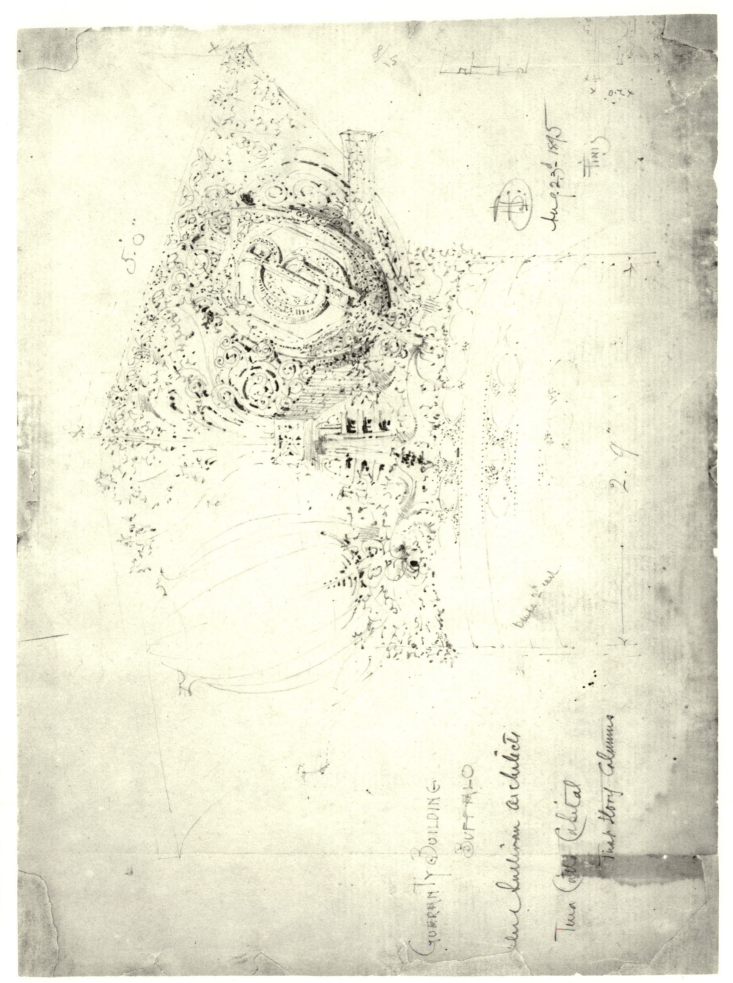

No. 99. Ornamental Capital, Guaranty Building, Buffalo, N.Y. Pencil. Louis Sullivan. August 23, 1895.

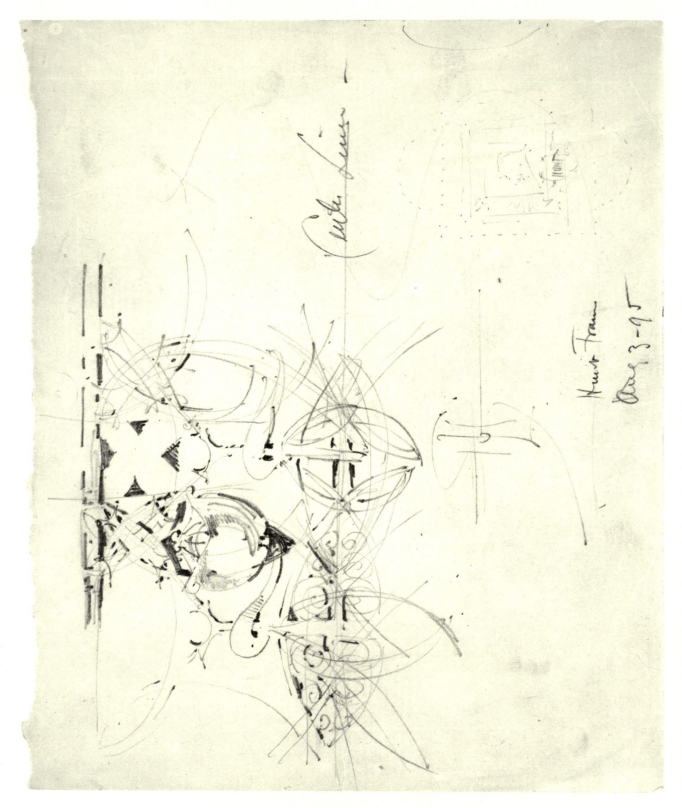

No. 100. Ornamental Frame for Hunt Memorial Page. Pencil. Louis Sullivan. August 3, 1895.

No. 101. Ornamental Design. Pencil.
Louis Sullivan. August 12, 1895.

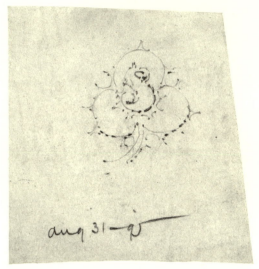

102

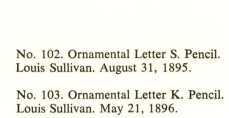

No. 102. Ornamental Letter S. Pencil.
Louis Sullivan. August 31, 1895.

No. 103. Ornamental Letter K. Pencil.
Louis Sullivan. May 21, 1896.

No. 104. Ornamental Letter B. Pencil.
Louis Sullivan. June 25, 1896.

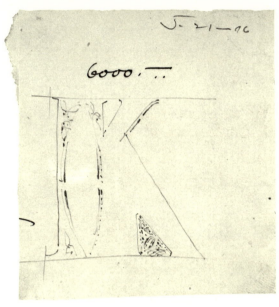

103

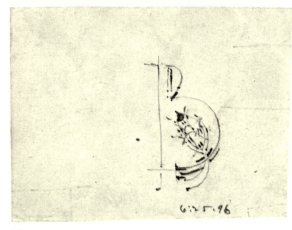

104

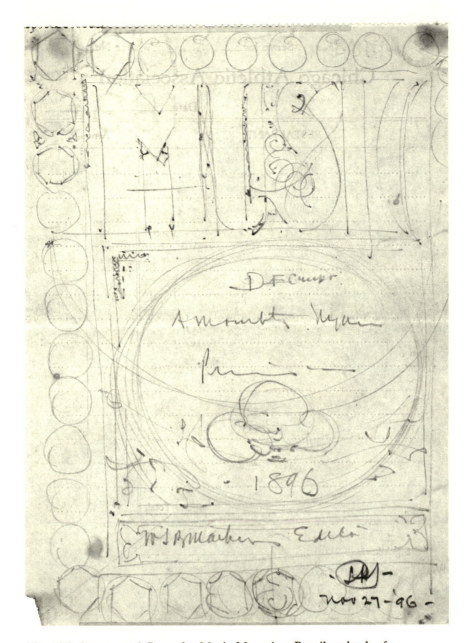

No. 105. Ornamental Cover for Music Magazine. Pencil on back of
Chicago Athletic Association restaurant check.
Louis Sullivan. November 27, 1896.

No. 106. Drawing of a Country Club. Pencil on the back of Sullivan's business card. Louis Sullivan. June 26, 1898.

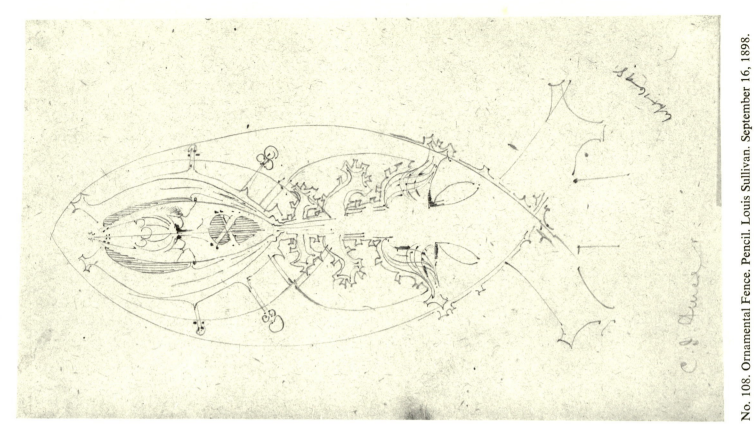

No. 108. Ornamental Fence. Pencil. Louis Sullivan. September 16, 1898.

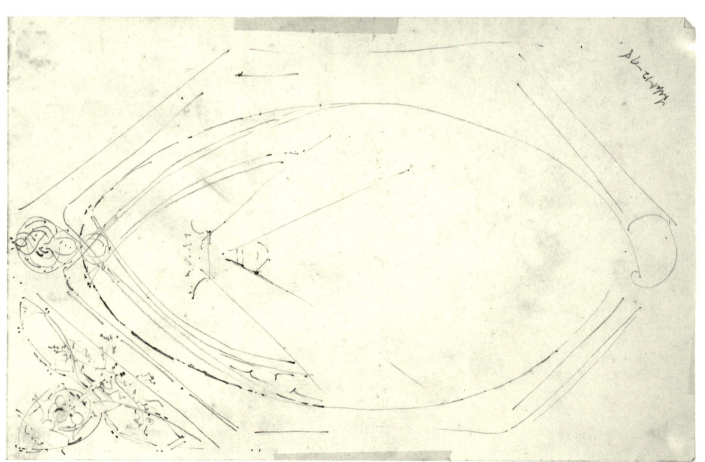

No. 107. Ornamental Design. Pencil. Louis Sullivan. September 12, 1898.

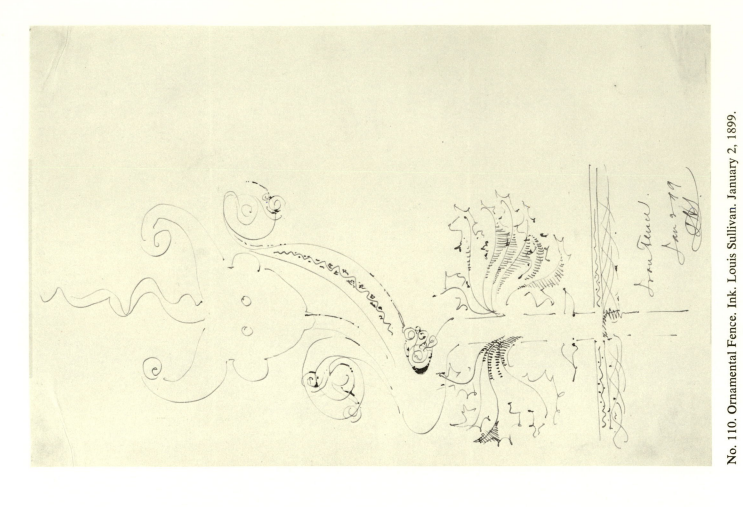

No. 110. Ornamental Fence. Ink. Louis Sullivan. January 2, 1899.

No. 109. Ornamental Fence. Ink. Louis Sullivan. January 2, 1899.

No. 112. Ornamental Design. Pencil. Louis Sullivan. January 26, 1899.

No. 111. Ornamental Design. Pencil on back of accounting paper with a two-cent stamp affixed to it. Louis Sullivan. January 10, 1899.

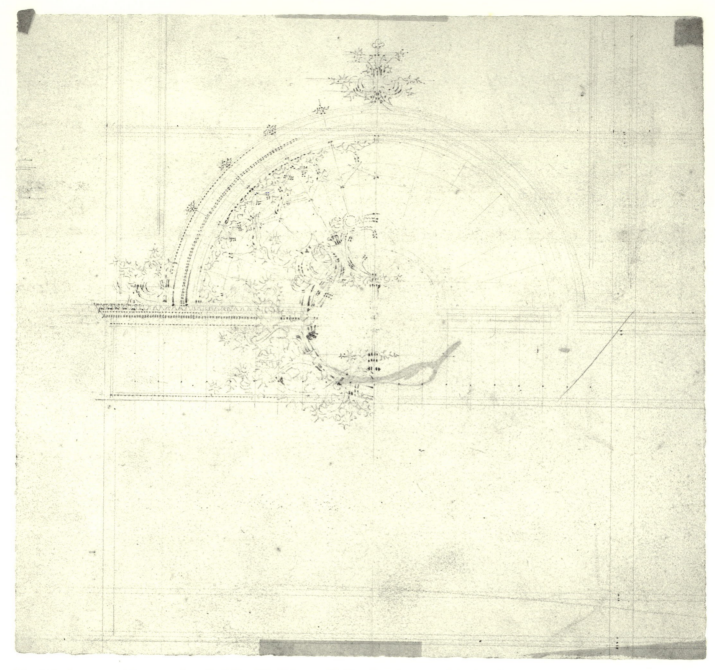

No. 113. Ornamental Lunette, Gage Building [?], Chicago, Ill. Pencil on heavy-weight drawing paper.
Louis Sullivan. c. 1899.

No. 114. Ornamental Iron Spandrel, Schlesinger & Mayer Building, Chicago, Ill. Pencil on heavy-weight drawing paper. Louis Sullivan. 1899.

No. 115. Ornamental Design. Pencil.
Louis Sullivan. April 2, 1902.

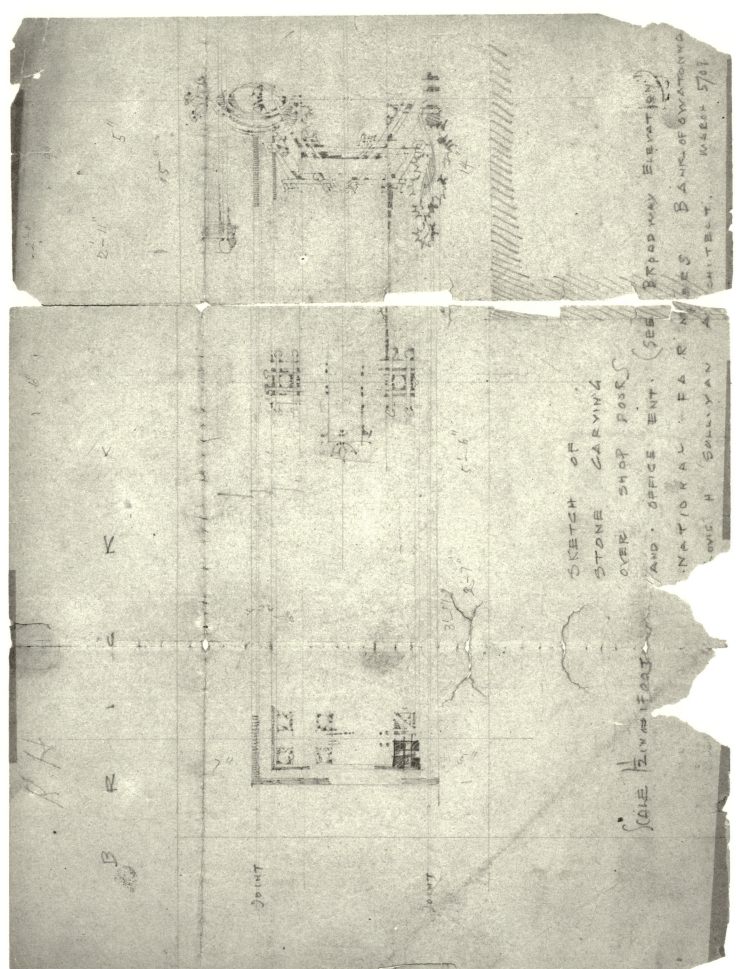

No. 116. Ornamental Panel, National Farmers' Bank, Owatonna, Minn. Pencil. Drawn by George Elmslie. March 5, 1907.

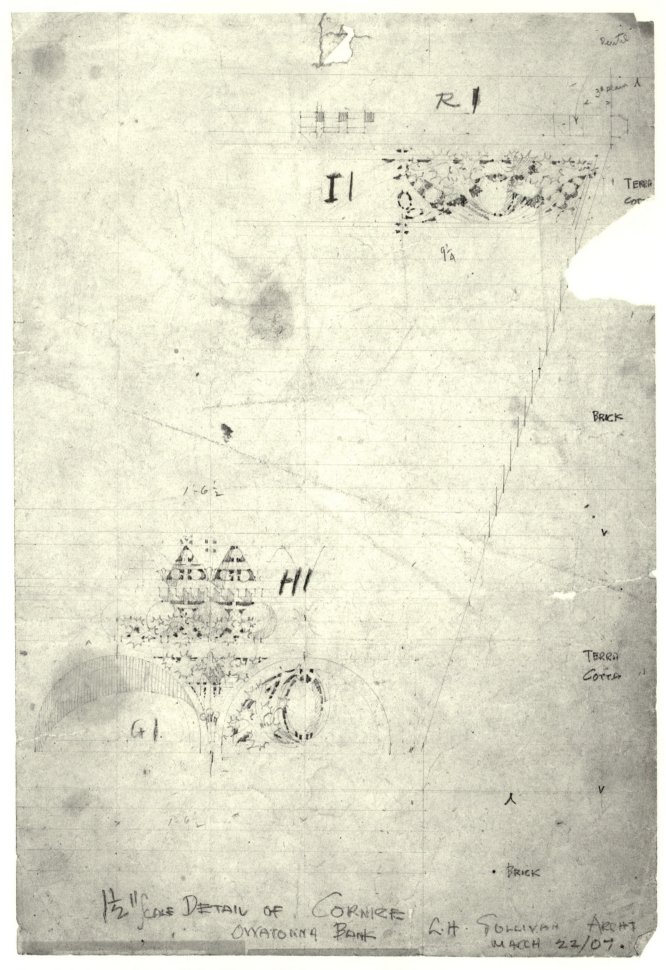

No. 117. Ornamental Cornice, National Farmers' Bank, Owatonna, Minn. Pencil.
Drawn by George Elmslie. March 22, 1907.

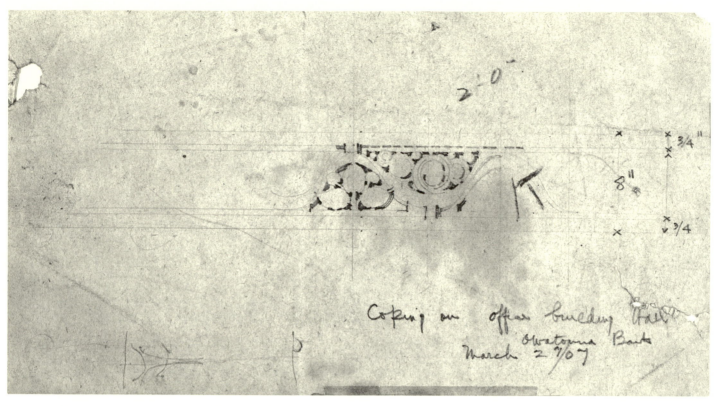

No. 118. Ornamental Coping, National Farmers' Bank, Owatonna, Minn. Pencil.
Drawn by George Elmslie. March 27, 1907.

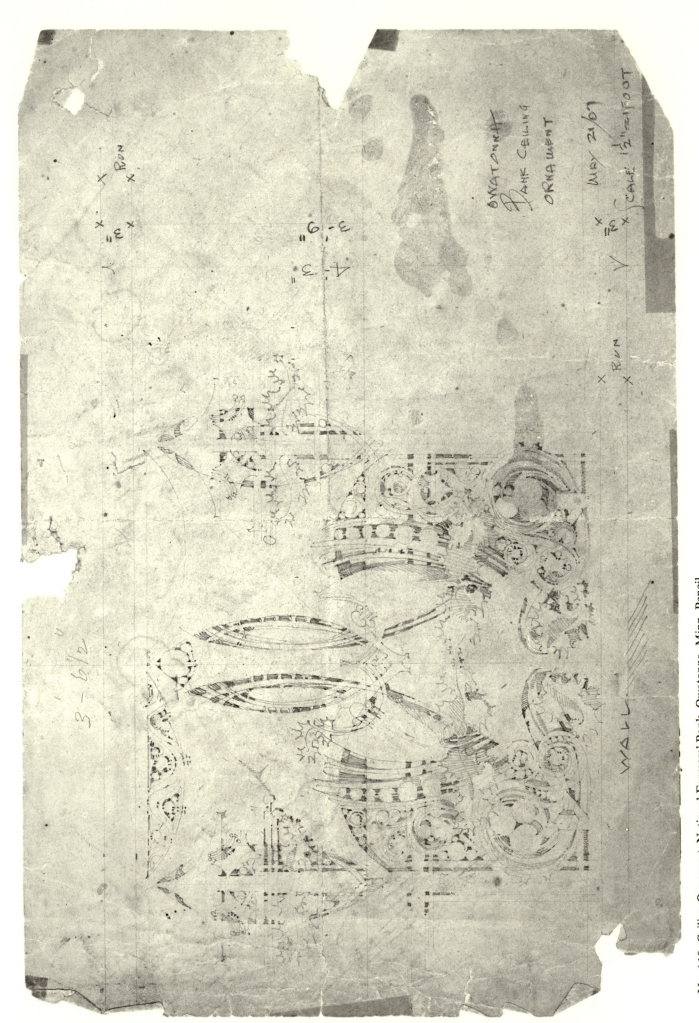

No. 119. Ceiling Ornament, National Farmers' Bank, Owatonna, Minn. Pencil.
Drawn by George Elmslie. May 21, 1907.

No. 120. Ornamental Clock Frame, National Farmers' Bank, Owatonna, Minn. Pencil.
Drawn by George Elmslie. June 12, 1907.

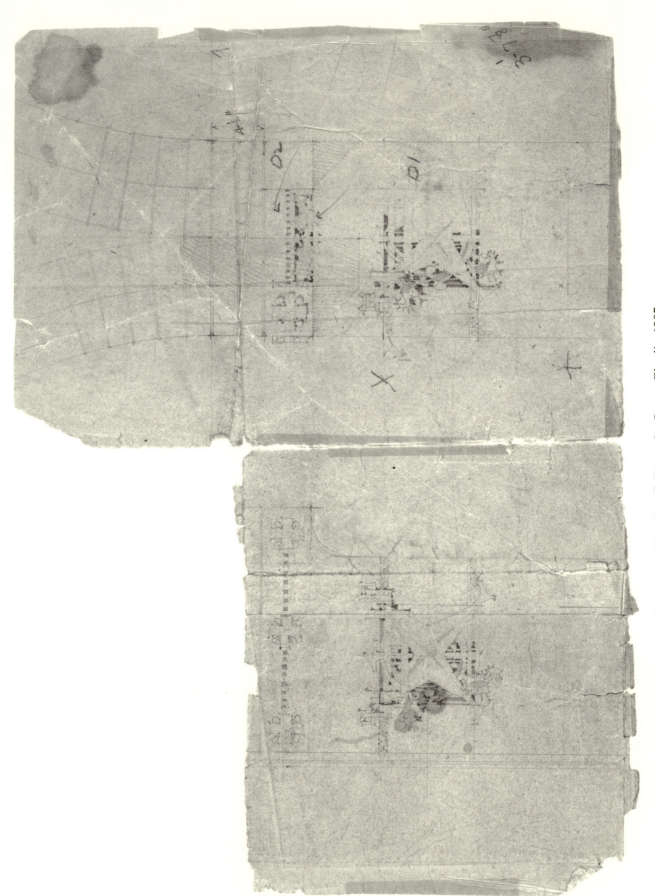

No. 121. Ornamental Pier, National Farmers' Bank, Owatonna, Minn. Pencil. Drawn by George Elmslie. 1907.

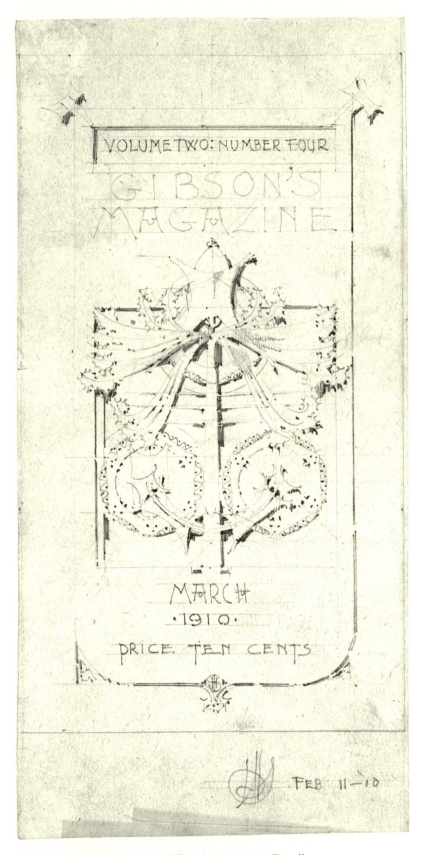

No. 122. Cover Design for *Gibson's Magazine*. Pencil.
Louis Sullivan. February 11, 1910.

COMPARATIVE ILLUSTRATIONS

Fig. 1. Chain Bridge, Newburyport, Mass. Pencil on paper. Andrienne Sullivan. 1867.

Fig. 2. Chain Bridge, Newburyport, Mass. Pencil on paper. Patrick Sullivan. 1868.

Fig. 3. Drawing of "Nouvelle Année" by Alfred Grévin from *Le Journal Amusant*, January 9, 1875, p. l. Ink on tracing paper. Louis Sullivan. March 15, 1875.

Fig. 4. Stone carving at entrance Digby Mortuary Chapel, Sherborne, Dorset, England. William Slater, architect. 1860.

Fig. 5. Interior stencil, St. James the Less, London, England. George E. Street, architect. c. 1860.

Fig. 6. Stone carving over window on front of the Pennsylvania Academy of Fine Arts.
Philadelphia, Penn. Frank Furness, architect. 1871-1876.

Fig. 7. Page from Furness Sketchbook. Pencil on paper.
Frank Furness. 1870-1880.

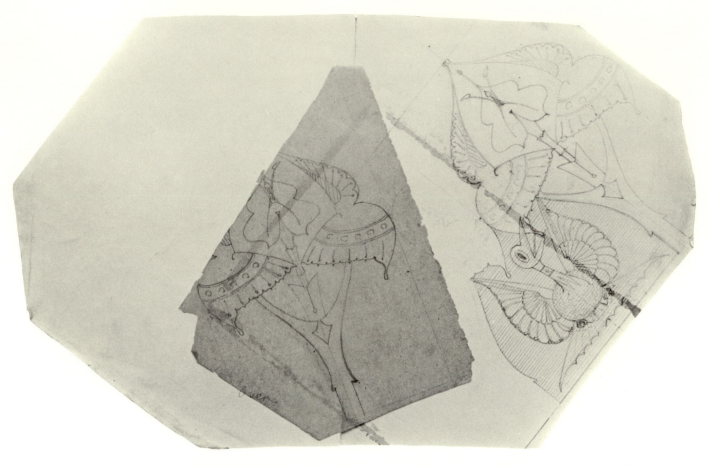

Fig. 8. Study for fresco design. Pencil on paper; pencil on tracing paper overlay. Louis Sullivan. 1874. Obverse of Fig. 9.

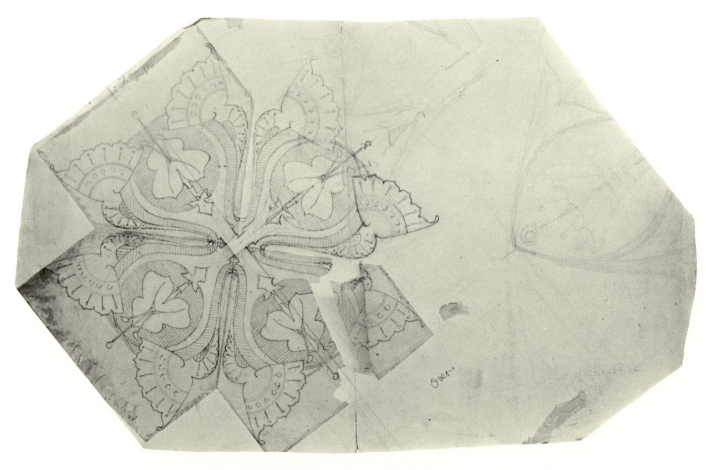

Fig. 9. Study for fresco design. Pencil on paper; pencil on tracing paper overlay. Louis Sullivan. 1874. Reverse of Fig. 8.

Fig. 10. Fresco design. Pencil on paper. Louis Sullivan. 1875.

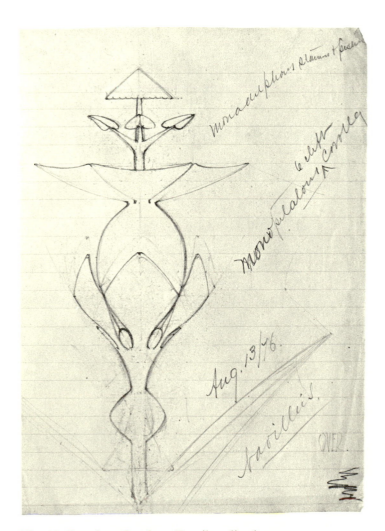

Fig. 11. Drawing of a plant. Pencil on lined paper.
Louis Sullivan. August 13, 1876.

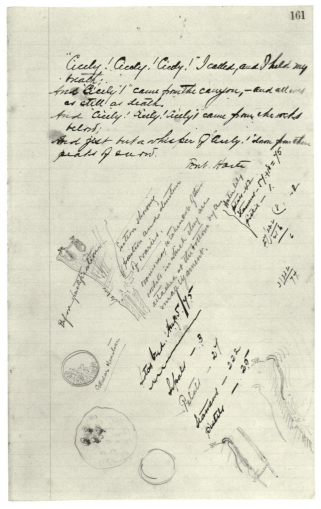

Fig. 12. Drawing of a Lotus Bud. Ink on lined paper
in Lotos Club Notebook, p. 161. Louis Sullivan.
August 5, 1875.

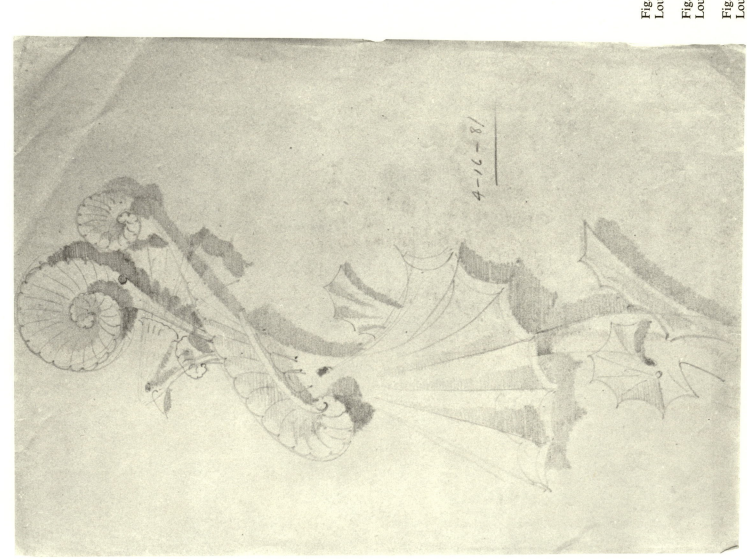

Fig. 13. Ornamental design. Pencil on paper.
Louis Sullivan. April 16, 1881.

Fig. 14. Drawing of various subjects. Pencil on paper.
Louis Sullivan. March 23, 1881.

Fig. 15. Drawing of a nude figure. Pencil on paper.
Louis Sullivan. December 25, 1879.

13

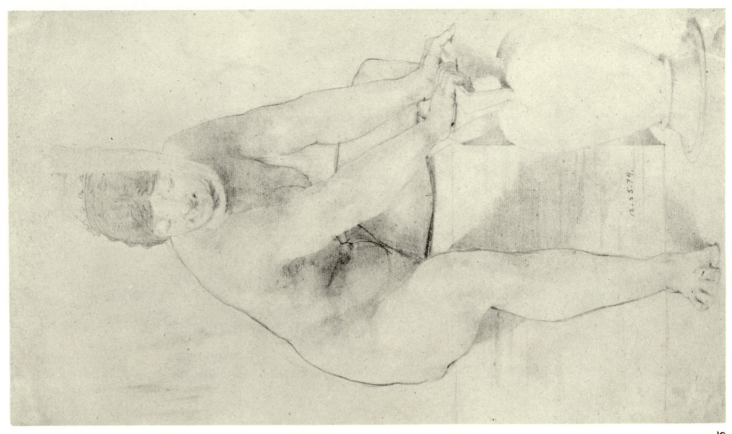

15

14

Fig. 16. Plaster corbel, Auditorium Building, Chicago, Ill. Adler & Sullivan, architects. 1888-1889.

Fig. 17. Mosaic stair landing between the first and second floors, Auditorium Building, Chicago, Ill. Adler & Sullivan, architects. 1888-1889.

Fig. 18. Mosaic stair landing between the second and third floors, Auditorium Building, Chicago, Ill. Adler & Sullivan, architects. 1888-1889.

Fig. 19. Wall mosaic, North inglenook, Auditorium Theater Lobby, Auditorium Building, Chicago, Ill. Adler & Sullivan, architects. 1888-1889.

Fig. 20. Drawing for a newel post, Auditorium Building, Chicago, Ill.
Adler & Sullivan, architects. 1888-1889.

Fig. 21. Newel post, Auditorium Building, Chicago, Ill. Adler & Sullivan, architects. 1888-1889.

Fig. 22. Capital of carved wood, Banquet Hall, Auditorium Building, Chicago, Ill.
Adler & Sullivan, architects. 1890.

Fig. 23. Capital of carved wood, Banquet Hall, Auditorium Building, Chicago, Ill.
Adler & Sullivan, architects. 1890.

Fig. 24. Capital of carved wood, Banquet Hall, Auditorium Building, Chicago, Ill.
Adler & Sullivan, architects. 1890.

Fig. 25. Terra-cotta ornamental panel. K.A.M. Synagogue, Chicago, Ill.
Adler & Sullivan, architects. 1890.

Fig. 26. Detail of stone cornice, Getty Tomb, Chicago, Ill. Adler & Sullivan, architects. 1890.

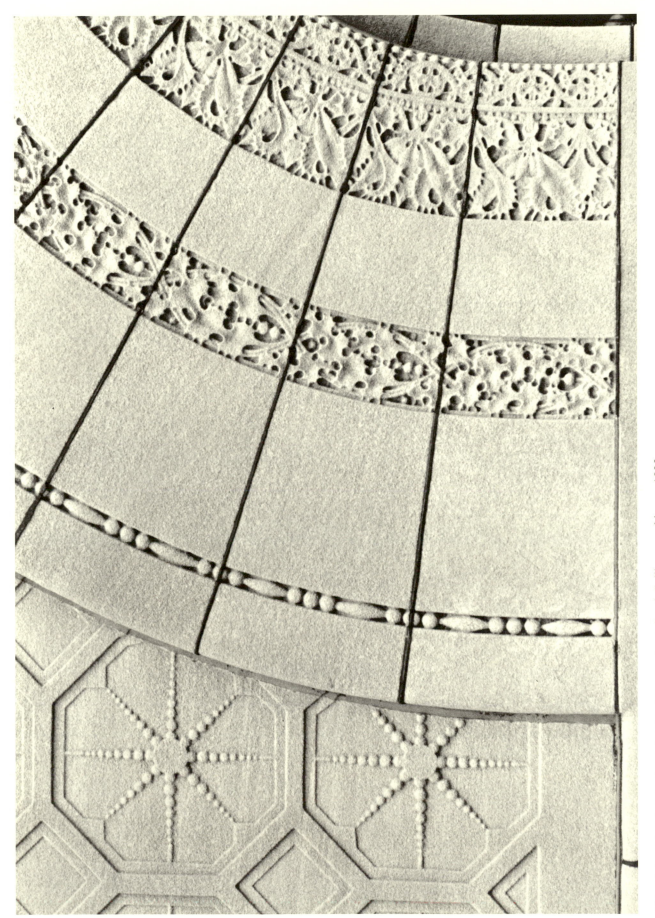

Fig. 27. Detail of facade, Getty Tomb, Chicago, Ill. Adler & Sullivan, architects. 1890.

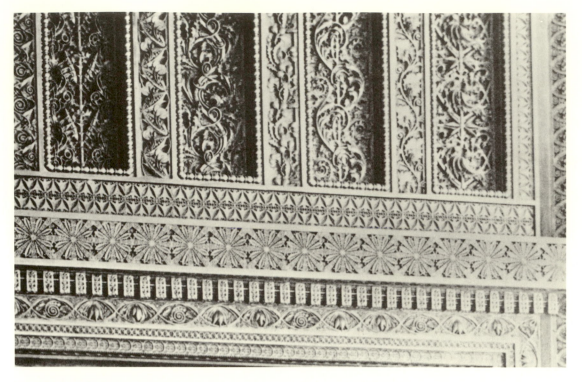

Fig. 28. Detail of plaster sounding board, McVicker's Theater, Chicago, Ill.
Adler & Sullivan, architects. 1890-1891.

Fig. 29. Detail of plaster spandrel of proscenium, K.A.M. Synagogue, Chicago, Ill.
Adler & Sullivan, architects, 1890-1891.

Fig. 30. Drawing for plaster ornament on sounding board, McVicker's Theater, Chicago, Ill. Adler & Sullivan, architects. 1890-1891.

Fig. 31. Drawing for plaster ornament on sounding board, McVicker's Theater, Chicago, Ill. Adler & Sullivan, architects. 1890-1891.

Fig. 32. Terra-cotta spandrel under seventh story line, Wainwright Building, St. Louis, Mo.
Adler & Sullivan and Ramsey, architects. 1890-1891.

Fig. 33. Plaster detail of main entrance, Transportation Building, Chicago, Ill.
Adler & Sullivan, architects. 1891-1892.

Fig. 34. Plaster details of fountain, Transportation Building, Chicago, Ill.
Adler & Sullivan, architects, 1891-1892.

Fig. 35. Stone carving over front door, Albert Sullivan House, Chicago, Ill.
Adler & Sullivan, architects. 1891-1892.

Fig. 36. Drawing for a limestone frieze, Wainwright Tomb, St. Louis, Mo. Louis Sullivan. 1892.

Fig. 37. Plaster capital, Exchange Room, Chicago Stock Exchange Building, Chicago, Ill. Adler & Sullivan, architects. 1894.

Fig. 38. Banquet Hall, St. Nicholas Hotel, St. Louis, Mo. Adler & Sullivan and Ramsey, architects. 1894.

Fig. 39. Terra-cotta and mosaic fireplace, Banquet Hall, St. Nicholas Hotel, St. Louis, Mo.
Adler & Sullivan and Ramsey, architects. 1894.

Fig. 40. Stencil on plaster, St. Nicholas Hotel, St. Louis, Mo. Adler & Sullivan and Ramsey, architects. 1894.

Fig. 41. Obverse of oratory medal. Louis Sullivan. 1895.

Fig. 42. Reverse of oratory medal. Louis Sullivan. 1895.

Fig. 43. Iron stair balusters, Guaranty Building, Buffalo, N.Y. Adler & Sullivan, architects. 1895.

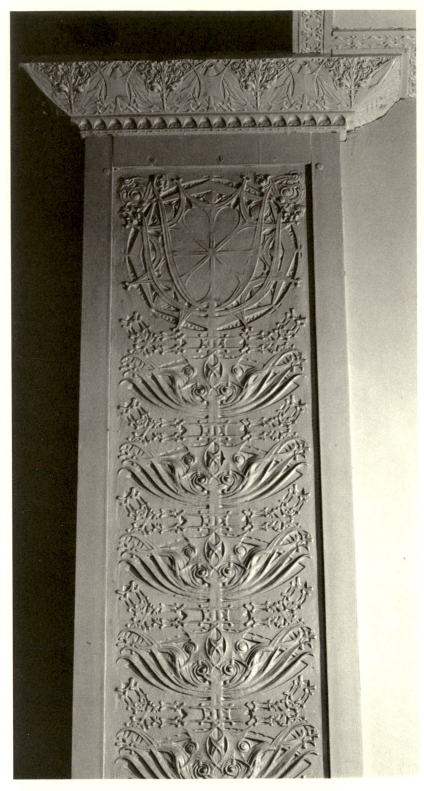

Fig. 44. Cast-iron pier, Guaranty Building, Buffalo, N.Y.
Adler & Sullivan, architects. 1895.

Fig. 45. Cast-iron door plate,
Guaranty Building, Buffalo, N.Y.
Adler & Sullivan, architects.
1895.

Fig. 46. Terra-cotta capital, Guaranty Building, Buffalo, N.Y. Adler & Sullivan, architects. 1895.

Fig. 47. Hunt memorial page, *Inland Architect*. Louis Sullivan. 1895.

Fig. 48. *Music* magazine cover. Louis Sullivan. 1896.

Fig. 49. Cast-iron spandrel, Schlesinger & Mayer Building, Chicago, Ill.
Louis Sullivan, architect. 1899.

Fig. 50. Terra-cotta pier, Office
Building, National Farmers' Bank,
Owatonna, Minn.
Louis Sullivan, architect. 1907.

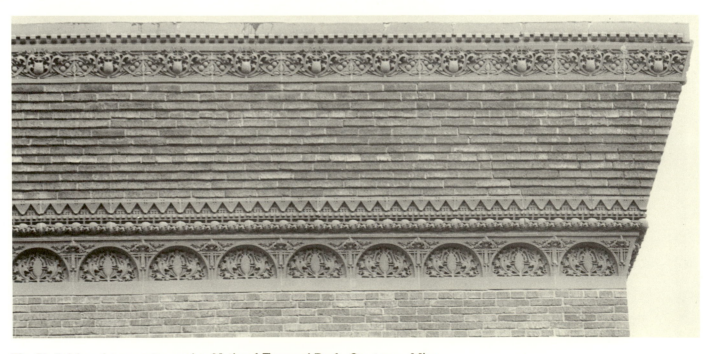

Fig. 51. Brick and terra-cotta cornice, National Farmers' Bank, Owatonna, Minn.
Louis Sullivan, architect. 1907.

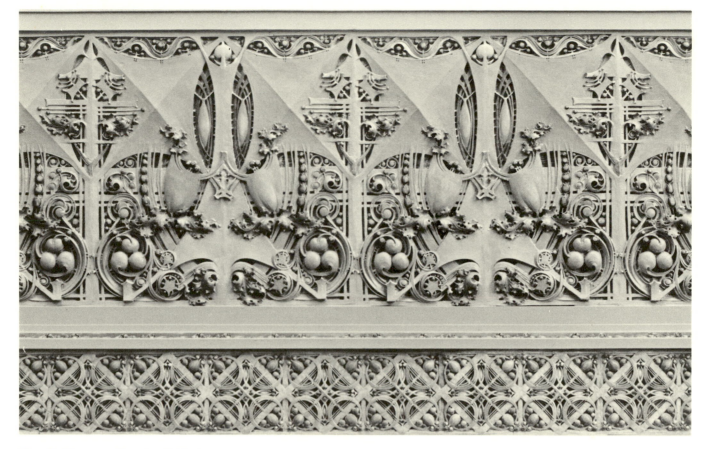

Fig. 52. Plaster ceiling detail, National Farmers' Bank, Owatonna, Minn.
Louis Sullivan, architect. 1907.

Fig. 53. Terra-cotta and bronze clock, National Farmers' Bank, Owatonna, Minn.
Louis Sullivan, architect. 1907.

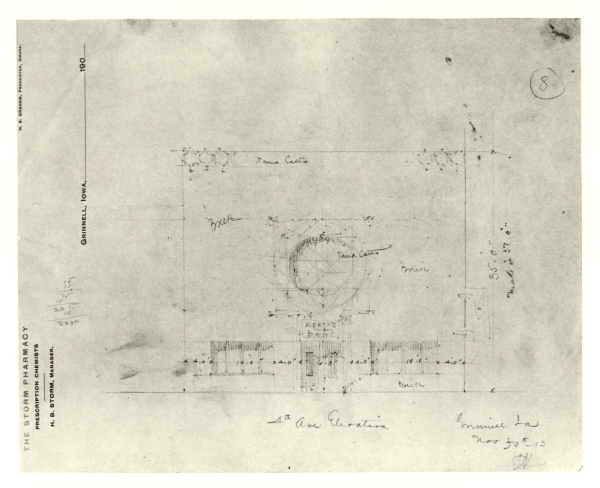

Fig. 54. Elevation of facade, Merchants' National Bank, Grinnell, Ia. Pencil on paper.
Louis Sullivan. November 30, 1913.

Fig. 55. Merchants' National Bank, Grinnell, Ia. Louis Sullivan. 1913-1914.

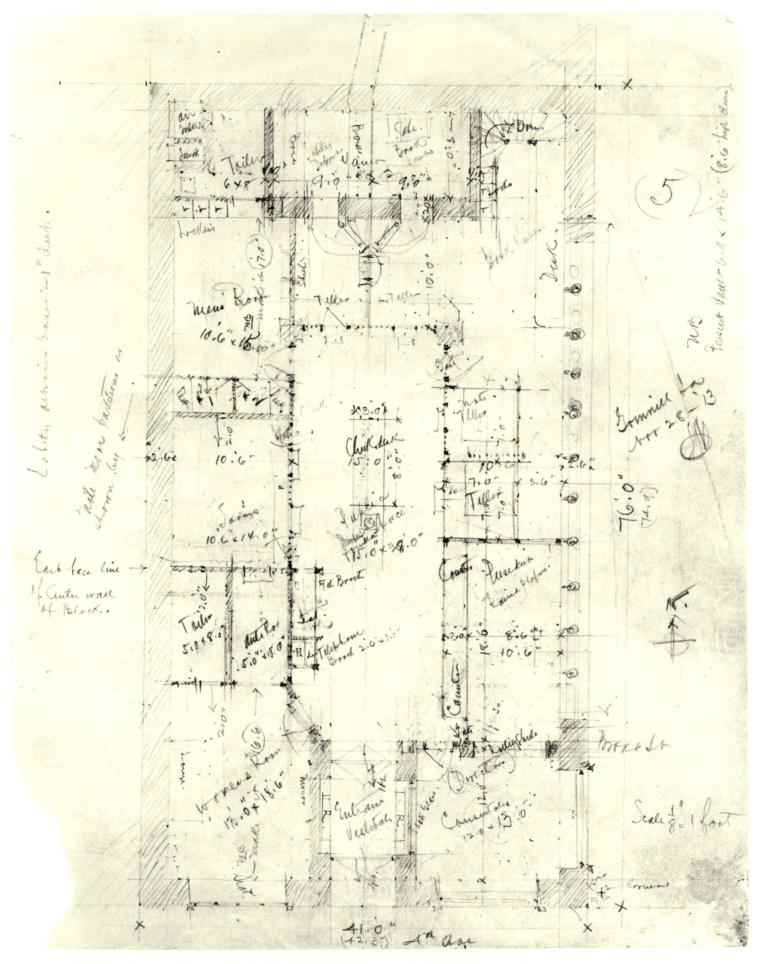

Fig. 56. Plan, Merchants' National Bank, Grinnell, Ia. Pencil on paper. Louis Sullivan.
November 28, 1913.

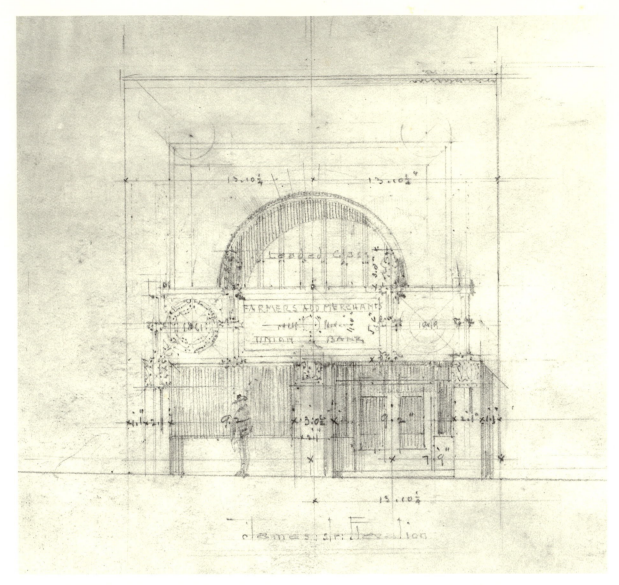

Fig. 57. Front elevation, Farmers' and Merchants' Union Bank, Columbus, Wis. Pencil on paper. Louis Sullivan. 1919.

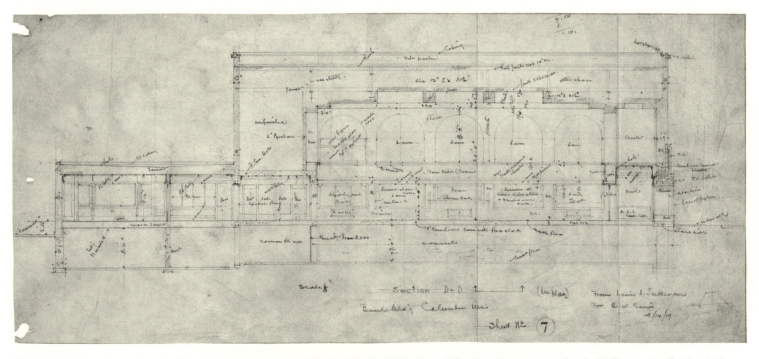

Fig. 58. Section through bank, Farmers' and Merchants' Union Bank, Columbus, Wis. Pencil on paper. Louis Sullivan. April 14, 1919.

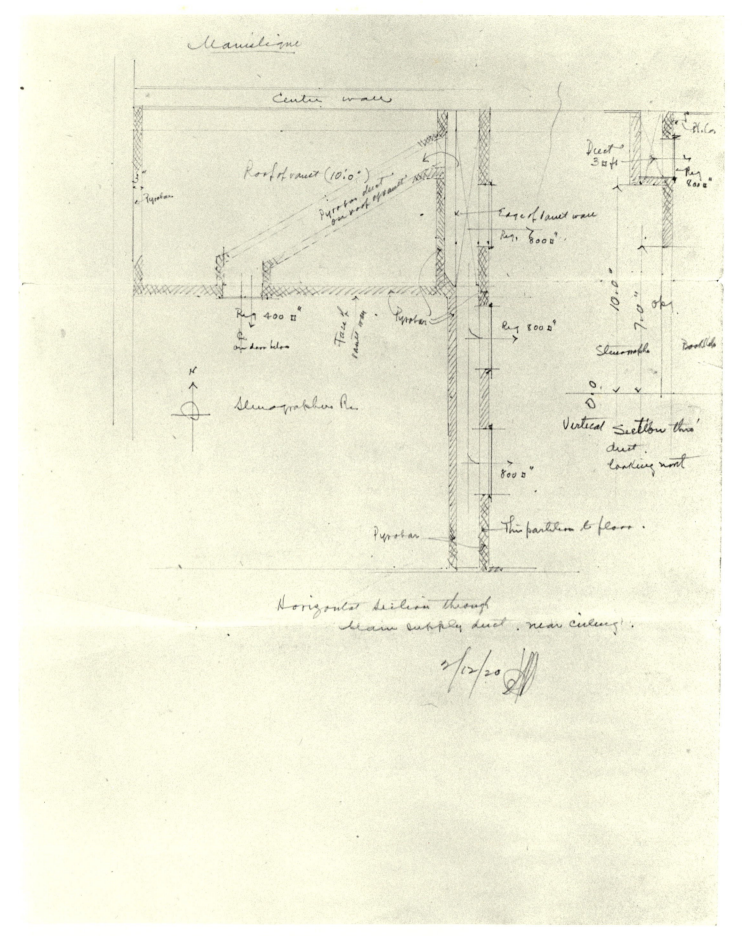

Fig. 59. Drawing for a bank at Manistique, Mich. Pencil on paper. Louis Sullivan.
February 12, 1920.

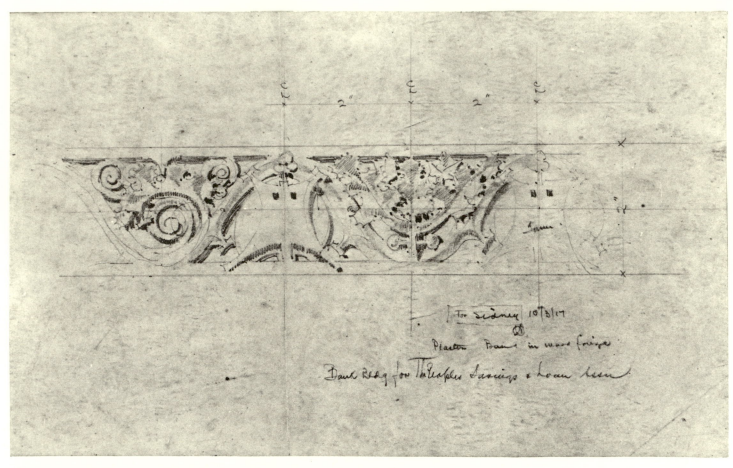

Fig. 60. Drawing for terra-cotta ornament, People's Savings & Loan Association, Sidney, Ohio.
Pencil on paper. Louis Sullivan. October 3, 1917.

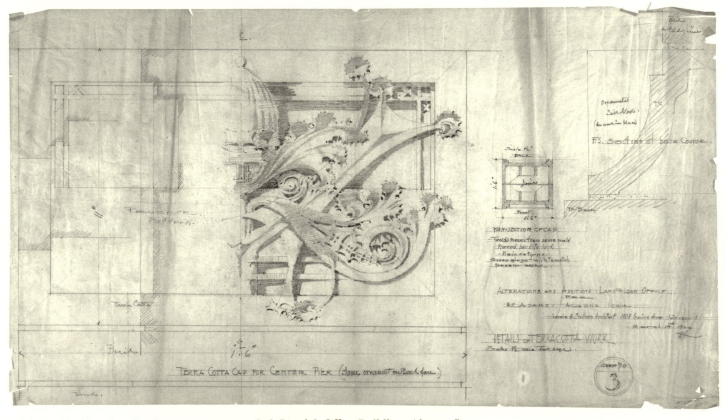

Fig. 61. Working drawing for a terra-cotta capital, Land & Office Building, Algona, Ia.
Pencil on tracing paper. Louis Sullivan. March 14, 1920.

Fig. 62. Drawing for George Nimmons. Louis Sullivan. September 25, 1918.

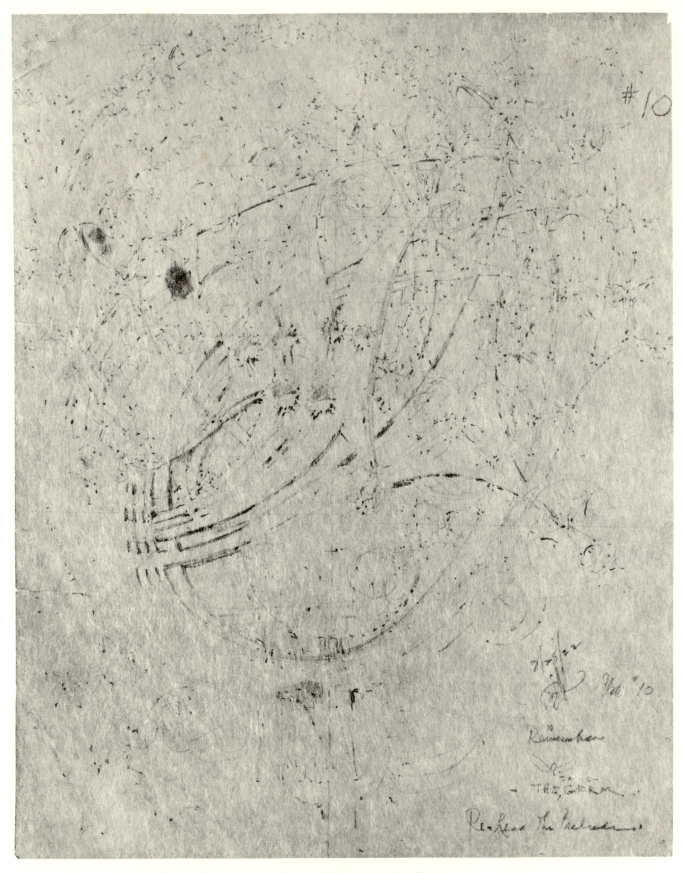

Fig. 63. Drawing for plate 10 of *A System of Architectural Ornament*. Pencil on paper.
Louis Sullivan. March 28, 1922.